40 DAYS
TO A LIFE OF
G.O.L.D.
(God-Ordained Life Development)

40 DAYS
TO A LIFE OF
G.O.L.D.
(God-Ordained Life Development)

Ed Gray

Judson Press ◆ Valley Forge

40 DAYS TO A LIFE OF G.O.L.D.
(GOD-ORDAINED LIFE DEVELOPMENT)

Library of Congress Cataloging-in-Publication Data
Gray, Ed, 1964-
    40 days to a life of G.O.L.D. : (God-ordained life development) / Ed Gray.
        p. cm.
    Includes bibliographical references.
    ISBN 0-8170-1463-2 (alk. paper)
    1. Christian life. I. Title: Forty days to a life of G.O.L.D. II. Title.
    BV4515.3.G73 2004
    248.4--dc22

                                                                2004004212

Printed in the U.S.A.

10 09 08 07 06 05
10 9 8 7 6 5 4 3 2

This book is dedicated to my mother, Essie Spencer, and my late father, Eddie Gray. Without the two of you, none of the work that God uses me for would be possible.

Mom, thank you for giving birth and helping to raise me. Your love and commitment have been continuous. You have more than earned my love and respect.

Dad, thank you for all that you gave while you were alive. You were a good man and a great father. I am most grateful for your love and the quality time you spent with me. It was a privilege to have a relationship with you.

CONTENTS

CONTENTS

FOREWORD

When Ed Gray asked me to contribute the foreword for this book, I agreed without hesitation for two reasons. First, I know that he *is* the message he brings. Second, I trained him.

I met Ed in 1989 when life was calling him to come up higher. He worked as a sales rep for a major corporation in Detroit while pursuing his dream of professional speaking. He used his sales skills and landed his first paid speaking engagement with Coca-Cola USA without any prior professional speaking experience. I was in town and speaking before the Black Aviators Association at the Ponchartrain Hotel in downtown Detroit. He came to me and said, "Les, I need your help. I just got my first speaking engagement, and I don't know what I am doing."

I admired his honesty and tenacity. I helped him with the design of that program, and it was a major success. The rest is history in the making.

Ed is one who continues to dig deep. He goes deep into the spiritual realm and pulls out rare and witty insights. His gifts can only be described as God-given.

Ed has grown tremendously from his first professional speaking engagement thirteen years ago to speaking at colleges, corporations, and churches all over the country. He grew quickly. I recall saying to Ed before doing my first PBS special, "The media are going to open a lot of doors for us." He believed me. I guess I was right. Less than a year after he began walking in his calling, he became a popular inspirational columnist for the *Michigan Chronicle* and was later picked up by the *Detroit News* and several other major newspapers.

This former student of mine has continued to follow in my footsteps. In 1991, when my schedule got so busy that I could no longer write and host the nationally syndicated radio feature *Power Minute,* Ed was a natural pick to continue the show.

From reading *40 Days to a Life of G.O.L.D. (God-Ordained Life Development),* I see that Ed has not stopped growing. This work has important spiritual substance. The acronyms make his ideas easy to digest, remember, and share with others.

The authors of the book *The Tipping Point* pointed out that "there is a simple way to package information that, under the right circumstances, can make it irresistible; all you have to do is find it." Ed has found the way. *40 Days to a Life of G.O.L.D.* is an irresistible magnet of truth that will draw many readers to a better understanding of God and themselves. It is an instant classic. As Ed would say, it's A.W.E.S.O.M.E. (As We Experience Spirit, Our Minds Expand).

I know you will enjoy reading this book as much as I have.

Les Brown
world-renowned motivational speaker
and best-selling author of
It's Not Over Until You Win!
and *Live Your Dreams*

ACKNOWLEDGMENTS

A special thanks goes to God for entrusting me with this assignment and blessing me with the necessary T.A.L.E.N.T.S. (Tools, Anointing/Ability, Love; Everything Needed To Succeed) in this work. I am honored that you chose me. I enjoy writing with you.

I would like to thank my agent, Dave Robie at BigScore Productions, as well as Randy Frame and all the wonderful people at Judson Press who made this book possible. Special thanks to Eric Stanford and Victoria McGoey; you both did an exceptional job.

I also wish to thank Barbara Robidoux at The Christian Communicator for reviewing and editing the original book proposal. A thanks also goes to Nancy McDaniel for editing and improving the original manuscript.

I want to thank pastors Robin Hancox and Calvin Tibbs of International Gospel Outreach in Smyrna, Georgia. Thanks also to my father in the ministry, the late Rev. Dr. Frederick G. Sampson of Tabernacle Missionary Baptist Church in Detroit, Michigan. Thank you for being a covering and not a lid. You saw my gifting and anointing and provided another platform for sharing it, encouraging me to enlarge my territory. Under your watch, you have encouraged my growth as a man and a minister of the gospel. You have given me the pastoral mentoring I need. To Sally Dean, Aretha Franklin (the other one, not the Queen of Soul), Adeniyi Adeniran, Angelo and Gloria Hunter, Belinda Poe, and Michelle Cooper, thank you for your prayers.

I would also like to express my thanks to Robert Sunday of Prophetic Prayer Ministries in Lagos, Nigeria.

I especially acknowledge my "big brother" Glen Davis. Your friendship, support, and belief in me over these last seventeen years have meant a lot. You've helped me get through some tough times, and you've been instrumental in helping to open some major doors. You are an exemplary model of friendship and Christian brotherhood.

A special thanks to Les Brown and George Fraser, whose shoulders I stand on as a foundation for inspirational speaking and writing. You both are unselfish in helping others, and I have been blessed because of you.

I would also like to thank Al Anderson, Virgil Scott, and Vanessa Vaughn at Anderson Communications. Through the years that I have written and hosted *Power Minutes,* you all have trusted and believed in the Christ within me.

I also wish to express my thanks to my dear friends Karen Dumas, Hundley (Attila) Batts, John and Nadine Jean-Pierre, José Alea, Angela Mason, Lisa Grass, Bob Hill, Omar Neal, Kelly McWilliams, Celeste Jonson, and Lisa Smith. I am grateful for your friendship.

I also give a hearty thanks to you, the reader, for purchasing this book. Use it to enter your Promised Land.

INTRODUCTION

Many of us spend most of our lives doing the but. "Doing the but" is making excuses. I hear them all the time: "I would have been rich, but ..." "I could have made something more of my life, but ..." Would have, could have, should have ... but, but, but. Excuses will put you into an uncomfortable rut. Time out for excuses! Your life is a gold mine filled with opportunities! You cannot afford to be hindered by your excuses any longer! Your delays can bring about God's denials.

God was trying to lead the children of Israel from the bondage of lack and limitation and into a place of affluence. God sent the leaders of each of the twelve tribes of Israel to survey the land God was giving to them. They reported back to Moses, "We went into the land where you sent us; and it certainly does flow with milk and honey.... Nevertheless, the people who live in the land are strong, and the cities are fortified and very large" (Numbers 13:27-28, NASB). Because of fear, they lied to Moses, their families, their friends, and themselves. They imagined themselves out of pursuing a higher life and tried to influence others to also accept less than their privilege. Instead of leaning on God's promises, they looked for and found reasons why they couldn't achieve what rightfully belonged to them. They refused to follow the G.O.L.D. (God-Ordained Life Directives) handed down from God through the prophets. As a result, access to the Promised Land was denied and they were destroyed.

The few who changed their ways and began to walk toward their destiny delayed their arrival by four decades. They could have passed through the wilderness to the Promised Land in forty days. However, because of "the but," they got stuck in a rut and wandered for forty long years.

Have you ever felt like you were in the wilderness? Do you feel like you are in a rut now? If so, how long have you been wandering? Are you clear on who you are, where you are going, and how you will get there? Is your perceived destiny the destiny that God has ordained for you? Do you want to experience the life of abundance that God has promised you?

40 Days to a Life of G.O.L.D. (God-Ordained Life Development) was written to aid you in drawing closer to God and uncovering the abundance placed within you through C.H.R.I.S.T. (Courageous Honesty Reaching Inside Spirit; Trusting/Transforming). Your life will begin to change over the next forty days as you internalize the message that God is speaking, memorize the acronyms and Scriptures, and answer the questions. A soul stretched by a forty-day divine experience can never regain its previous limited dimension.

Don't be surprised if God decides to download witty inventions and ideas into your spirit and even shows you how to manifest them. You will not be disappointed in taking the journey that's before you. As God told the captives in Babylon,

When you come looking for me, you'll find me.

Yes, when you get serious about finding me and want it more than anything else, I'll make sure you won't be disappointed.

—Jeremiah 29:13, The Message

The captives were set free from their limiting circumstances. Do you want to be set free?

To get the most out of this book, read it with your spouse and/or a circle of friends, and discuss with each other what God is saying to you individually and collectively. Get together over coffee or dinner once a week and share what God is showing you. Jesus will indeed share in your discussions. "For where two or three come together in my name, there am I with them" (Matthew 18:20, NIV).

Over the next forty days, make a sacrifice by giving up something you enjoy. Some forces that hold us back can only be removed through fasting and prayer (Matthew 17:21). When I took my forty-day journey, I gave up coffee and sweets, which I enjoy immensely. I studied, meditated, and prayed. God revealed to me the direction and instructions to arrive at my destiny spiritually and professionally. I was not disappointed. Be led by the Holy Spirit in what you will give up as you begin your journey—in the end you will not be disappointed.

Are you willing to make the commitment? Open your calendar and schedule a daily appointment to spend fifteen to thirty minutes reading and meditating. Sign the G.O.L.D. (God-Ordained Life Development) Commitment and have your spouse and/or friends endorse your commitment as well. Be careful to honor your word.

MY G.O.L.D.
(God-Ordained Life Development)
COMMITMENT

I commit to investing adequate time each day to reading *40 Days to a Life of G.O.L.D. (God-Ordained Life Development)*. My aim is to develop a closer relationship with God. Lord Jesus, I invite you to come into my midst and help me grow stronger in you so that I can better serve others.

Signed this _____ day of _____ 20_____.

_____

Your signature

_____

Partner 1 signature

_____

Partner 2 signature

Getting your priorities right

DAY 1

P urpose
R equires
I mpartation
O f
R evelation;
I t
T eaches/Transforms
Y ou

Let God transform you into a new person by changing the way you think. Then you will know what God wants you to do.

−Romans 12:2, NLT

Upon hearing that someone has great potential, most people tend to think positively. We think that good things lie ahead for the person with potential, whether he or she aspires to be a great musician, a writer, an athlete, a teacher, or something else.

Upon closer examination, however, the word "potential" for some might have negative associations. "Potential" implies that something is lacking. It suggests that there is room for growth, for change, for a higher level of maturity or achievement. With mere potential, the reality is not as good as it might be or ought to be. People with potential, by definition, have not yet arrived at the places they want to be in their lives or in their careers. And there are no guarantees they ever will arrive.

As with other areas of life, our spiritual lives are full of potential, overflowing with possibilities. The challenge that lies before us constantly revolves around how we can realize or fulfill this potential. How do we turn what is possible into something real?

Fulfilling your potential as a child of God begins with uncovering the gifts and purposes for which God has designed you and to which God has called you. You may have your own ideas about your purposes and goals, but sometimes our priorities are not God's priorities. Your ideas for pursuing your purpose preexist in your mind like seeds in the ground. But for any idea to develop, God must fertilize it.

I believe that the process of discovering God's purpose for our lives is built around an attitude of praise, for God inhabits the praises of God's people (Psalm 22:3; Isaiah 61:10-11). "To praise" means "to set a price on." When you praise God, setting the highest value on your relationship with God, then God enters your heart and mind and fertilizes your ideas. If your purpose is to help others realize the power that is within them, God may fertilize your idea to write a book, as God did with the book you are now reading. Several years later, what you and God have grown together may influence more people than you could have ever imagined.

If your purpose is to be a good parent, God will fertilize your idea, and a great mother or father will be born. As a result, the children you parent have the opportunity to reflect a godly upbringing.

Most of us have a lot of ideas, both for our personal lives and for our career paths. I have ideas of marrying the woman of God's choosing and sharing my life with her, providing for her, making her happy, and raising a godly family. I have ideas of opening coffeehouses, producing television and radio programs, traveling the world, building training centers for the homeless, writing books, plays, movies, and much more. Although these ideas are in my mind, an impartation from God is necessary to fertilize any one of them. That is why being in relationship with God is a priority.

"To impart" means "to make known." If you seek to be close to God, God will make known to you the best way of bringing your ideas to fruition. God promised, "I will instruct you and teach you in the way you should go" (Psalm 32:8, NIV). God will guide each step of the way. God will even lead you to the financial resources and to the people who are needed to bring your ideas to fruition one at a time.

God has worked this way for thousands of years. Remember that about 3 million people left Egypt, but only a few families entered the Promised Land. Those who entered were the ones who sought God's purpose. The others were destroyed because they wanted to do things their way instead of God's way. In spite of the fact that God had given them revelation, they chose to disobey.

The same principle applies to our ideas. You can try to give life to a good idea by doing things your way, and you may discover (as I have on occasion) that a good idea that did not include God rarely sees the light of day. Even if it does, it is short-lived. But an idea born of God will always bear fruit, regardless of the obstacles you might face. Your role is to remain committed.

As you draw closer to God and God begins to fertilize your ideas, your life can change. But if these ideas are to reach their full potential, you must follow through. Oftentimes, this will not be easy. There will be roadblocks, hurdles, detractors. Even knowing that God has given birth to an idea, we may still be too used to doing things our own way instead of God's way.

Your thinking may have to change. As Jesus said, "[People do not] pour new wine into old wineskins. If they do, the skins will burst, the wine will run out and the wineskins will be ruined. No, they pour new wine into new wineskins, and both are preserved" (Matthew 9:17, NIV).

How do you get a new container to carry God's fresh ideas? "Let God transform you into a new person by changing the way you think. Then you will know what God wants you to do" (Romans 12:2, NLT).

If you are serious about fulfilling your life's mission, let Romans 12:2 be your P.R.I.O.R.I.T.Y. (Purpose Requires Impartation Of Revelation; It Teaches/Transforms You). As you will learn in tomorrow's lesson, your priorities must be in order; otherwise, you will always be in N.E.E.D. (Not Enough Energy; Dead).

Acronym to Remember: **P.R.I.O.R.I.T.Y.**
(**P**urpose **R**equires **I**mpartation **O**f **R**evelation; **I**t **T**eaches/ **T**ransforms **Y**ou)

Verse to Remember:
"Let God transform you into a new person by changing the way you think. Then you will know what God wants you to do" (Romans 12:2, NLT).

4

Questions of the Day:

• What impartation or revelation did you receive from God in today's reading?

• What God-ideas do you possess?

• What steps of faith can you take so that God can show you how to manifest those ideas?

• What did you learn from today's reading, and with whom can you share it?

DAY 2

N ot
E nough
E nergy;
D ead

My God shall supply all your need according to his riches in glory by Christ Jesus.

–Philippians 4:19, KJV

A corporate executive had a $135,000 annual salary. With bonuses, he earned over $200,000 a year. Such earnings seem like a lot of money to most people, but it was not enough for this executive and many others like him.

He worked hard to provide for his family. In his work he traveled extensively. There were many nights when he was not home to tuck in his children and kiss them goodnight. Sometimes he missed his son's ball games. These are just a couple of the many sacrifices he made to afford his lifestyle.

The family lived in a gorgeous home in an upscale area. He drove a Porsche, and his wife drove a BMW. His children went to private schools, which cost him over $36,000 a year. In spite of his high earnings, he never seemed to have enough money. He was deep in debt, maxed out on his credit cards, and had recently suffered some serious investment losses.

Although his earnings might have been higher than ours, this guy was like most of us. With his higher income came more expensive tastes. He earned more than he had ten years earlier, but his stress was greater. With his job came more responsibility, and his job security was uncertain. There were rumors that the company was going to be sold. He wondered how he would afford his family's lifestyle if he were let go. He had become dependent upon his salary. Nevertheless, he hated his job.

This man had felt a call to the ministry many years ago. However, he had found the salaries of ministers insufficient to finance his dreams. He chose to get an MBA rather than go to seminary. By the standards of many, he was a success. Deep inside, however, he knew better.

He thought money would make him happy, but his unhappiness led him to heavy drinking and the use of antidepressant drugs. One day he cried out to the Lord, "What should I do?"

Now this is what the Lord Almighty says: Give careful thought to your ways. You have planted much, but harvested little. You eat, but you never have enough. You drink, but never have your fill. You put on clothes, but are not warm. You earn wages, only to put them in a purse with holes in it.

—Haggai 1:5-6, NIV

What does God mean by "Give careful thought to your ways"? The Sermon on the Mount suggests an answer.

Do not worry about your life, what you will eat; or about your body, what you will wear. Is not life more important than food, and the body more important than clothes? Look at the birds of the air; they do not sow or reap or store away in barns, and yet your heavenly Father feeds them. Are you not much more valuable than they? Who of you by worrying can add a single hour to his life?

—Matthew 6:25-27, NIV

God gave each of us a job to do; that's why Jesus worked diligently while he was here on earth. He said, "My meat is to do the will of him that sent me, and to finish his work" (John 4:34, KJV). "Meat" refers to one's spiritual, physical, emotional, and financial substance. Provisions for everything you need and want are dependent upon doing what God has called you to do. If you do something other than what God has ordained for you to do, you will find yourself lacking in some important area of your life.

People who choose money instead of God's calling always short-change themselves. If God wants to make you rich, God can make you rich doing anything.

Your quality of life is greater if you are doing what God has called you to do and if you are doing it in the manner that God tells you to. "For the pagans run after all these things, and your heavenly Father knows

7

that you need them. But seek first his kingdom and his righteousness, and all these things will be given to you as well" (Matthew 6:32-34, NIV).

This truth is difficult to grasp for most of us as adults. However, it is so simple that even a child can understand. One of my favorite lines in the 1993 movie *Philadelphia* occurs when Denzel Washington, playing an attorney, says to an expert witness on the stand, "Explain it to me like I am a twelve-year-old child."

A class of children grasped the meaning of "Seek ye first the kingdom of God" when I taught them a lesson on values. I asked the children, "If God came to you and said, 'I will give you anything you want and as much of it as you want,' what would you ask for?"

The majority of the class said money. At the bottom of the chalkboard, I wrote the word "Money."

I then asked, "How do most people get money?"

They all said, "Work."

I placed the word "Work" above the word "Money" on the chalkboard.

Next I asked, "How do most people find work?"

They discussed this among themselves. The children who were aware of how their parents found jobs said, "Through family or friends." I articulated their answer on the chalkboard by writing the word "Contacts" above the word "Work."

I asked the children, "What would be the likelihood of an unemployed high-school dropout having friends who are lawyers or doctors?"

They agreed that it was improbable.

I then asked, "How does one find contacts?"

One child said by going to school. Another child said through joining organizations. I articulated their answers on the board by writing "Education/Skill" above the word "Contacts."

I asked the children, "How do you acquire an education or skill?"

They said, "Study or practice." I wrote "Study/Practice" above the words "Education/Skill."

"What causes a person to study or practice?"

The children said, "Desire."

I explained to them that the word *desire*, in its Latin root, means "from the Father." I then asked, "Where does desire come from?"

They said, "From God."

The list looked like this:

1. God
2. Desire
3. Study/Practice
4. Education/Skill
5. Contacts
6. Work
7. Money

Notice that money—the thing that most of us put first in our lives—is the last of the byproducts of seeking the kingdom of God and God's righteousness.

In the 1983 movie *Scarface,* Al Pacino's character, Tony Montana, reflects the world's attitude toward success. He says, "First you get the money, then you get the power, then you get the girl." That approach is backward and leads to death, mentally, spiritually, and (in Montana's case) physically.

The right approach is to seek the kingdom of God and God's righteousness, and all those things will be added unto you if they are meant for you. To seek God's kingdom, you have to go inside yourself (Luke 17:20-21), discover what God ordained you to do, and pursue it according to God's ways. God will provide for your needs and most of your wants.

Ralph Waldo Emerson understood this when he said, "Cause and effect, means and ends, seed and fruit, cannot be severed; for the effect already blooms in the cause, the end preexists in the means, the fruit in the seed."[1]

Perhaps you were doing as I once was—doing what is convenient, instead of what is ordained. As a result, God may have dried up the source of your income, and you lost your job. God allows this to happen when we are more focused on building our kingdom than we are on building God's kingdom.

---

1. *Ralph Waldo Emerson. From "Compensation," in* Emerson's Essays, *74. Copyright 1926 by Thomas Y. Crowell Company, Inc. Permission to reprint granted by Harper-Collins Publishers.*

It happened in the prophet Haggai's day. God told the people, "My house . . . remains a ruin, while each of you is busy with his own house. Therefore, because of you the heavens have withheld their dew and the earth its crops. I called for a drought on the fields and the mountains, on the grain, the new wine, the oil and whatever the ground produces" (Haggai 1:9-11, NIV).

Sometimes God allows things to go awry in our lives to give us another chance to do what God has placed us on this earth to do. God takes away our options. Some of us get the message, while others of us just wither up and die without completing our earthly assignments.

The corporate executive I mentioned earlier put his own dreams above God's calling on his life. He earned a decent living, but it was never enough. His soul was dead. "What will it profit a man if he gains the whole world and forfeits his soul? Or what will a man give in exchange for his soul?" (Matthew 16:26, NASB).

Do what God has called you to do, and you will never complain again about what you N.E.E.D. (Not Enough Energy; Dead).

**Acronym to Remember: N.E.E.D.
(Not Enough Energy; Dead)**

Verse to Remember:
"My God shall supply all your need according to his riches in glory by Christ Jesus" (Philippians 4:19, KJV).

Questions of the Day:
• What vocation have you felt led by God to pursue?

- Are you passionate about your present work?

- If not, what has stopped you from pursuing your passion?

- In your own words, explain why seeking first the kingdom of God and its righteousness is most important.

DAY 3

T ools,
A bility/Anointing,
L ove;
E verything
N eeded
T o
S ucceed

> Give her a share in the fruit of her hands,
> and let her works praise her in the city gates.
>
> —Proverbs 31:31, NRSV

Without a vocation, man's existence would be meaningless. We have been created to bear the responsibility God has entrusted us with. Though different, each man should fulfill his specific vocation and shoulder his individual responsibility. To do this he should first recognize and be loyal to his real entity within, regardless of any external factors; for it is this alone which will enable him to belong and owe allegiance to that Entity which is greater, vaster and more permanent than his individual self.[1]

—Anwar El-Sadat

Each of us has at least one thing that we can do better than anyone else in the world. No one could paint like Michelangelo. Although God had given others the gift of painting, Michelangelo's style was all his own. No one could write with the sensitivity, beauty, and depth of William Shakespeare. Shakespeare's place in history was reserved for him. No one can sing like

---

1. *Anwar El-Sadat*, In Search of Identity: An Autobiography, *82. Copyright 1977, 1978 by The Village of Milt Abul-Kum. English Translation copyright 1977, 1978 by Harper & Row Publishers. Permission to reprint granted by HarperCollins.*

Patti LaBelle. Sure, there are many others with strong voices and high energy, but there is only one Patti.

Finding your calling is a matter of exercising your faith. Comparable to the kingdom of God, it is "like a man going on journey, who called his servants and entrusted his property to them."

To one he gave five talents of money, to another two talents, and to another one talent, each according to his ability. Then he went on his journey. The man who had received the five talents went at once and put his money to work and gained five more. So also, the one with the two talents gained two more. But the man who had received the one talent went off, dug a hole in the ground and hid his master's money.

After a long time the master of those servants returned and settled accounts with them. The man who had received the five talents brought the other five. "Master," he said, "you entrusted me with five talents. See, I have gained five more."

His master replied, "Well done, good and faithful servant! You have been faithful with a few things; I will put you in charge of many things. Come and share your master's happiness!"

The man with the two talents also came. "Master," he said, "you entrusted me with two talents; see, I have gained two more."

His master replied, "Well done, good and faithful servant. You have been faithful with a few things; I will put you in charge of many things. Come and share your master's happiness!"

Then the man who had received the one talent came. "Master," he said, "I knew that you are a hard man, harvesting where you have not sown and gathering where you have not scattered seed. So I was afraid and went out and hid your talent in the ground. See, here is what belongs to you."

His master replied, "You wicked, lazy servant! So you knew that I harvest where I have not sown and gather where I have not scattered seed? Well then, you should have put my money on deposit with the bankers, so that when I returned I would have received it back with interest.

"Take the talent from him and give it to the one who has the ten talents. For everyone who has will be given more, and he will have abundance. Whoever does not have, even what he has will be taken from him. And throw that worthless servant outside, into the darkness, where there will be weeping and gnashing of the teeth."

—Matthew 25:14-30, NIV

The worthless servant was sent to hell.

The word *hell* comes from the Old English root word *helan*, meaning "limited." We create our hells and shut ourselves off from success by being afraid to fully exercise our talents, as did the servant who had the one talent. As a result, we weep about not having enough. We allege that life is unfair. We gnash our teeth in anger at those who have less talent than we do but more success and happiness.

Those whom God blesses are the ones who have faith. The servant given five talents and the servant given two talents exercised their faith and increased their substance. Their abundance was the evidence of their faith. "According to your faith be it unto you" (Matthew 9:29, KJV).

Faith is different from belief. Active faith is a matter of being trustworthy, reliable, and dependable. The foundation of faith is character. God is not going to take you to a level where your character cannot keep you. "Moreover it is required in stewards, that a man be found faithful" (1 Corinthians 4:2, KJV). A steward is someone whom God has entrusted. God has given each of us at least one talent; this makes us stewards.

"Much is required from those to whom much is given, for their responsibility is greater" (Luke 12:48, TLB). The more talent and opportunity you have been given, the more God expects of you. So that you will better understand how this applies to you, let's take a closer look at talents.

The T in *talent* stands for "tools." A tool is a resource that you use to perform a task. "Our tools are ready at hand for clearing the ground of every obstruction and building lives of obedience into maturity" (2 Corinthians 10:4, The Message). There are three tools that believers need to become proficient in using to fully utilize their gifts and complete their divine assignment.

The first tool is the Word of God. The Bible describes people who trust in the Word as blessed.

They delight in doing everything God wants them to, and day and night are always meditating on his laws and thinking about ways to follow him more closely.

They are like trees along a river bank bearing luscious fruit each season without fail. Their leaves shall never wither, and all they do shall prosper.

—Psalm 1:2-3, TLB

You must be focused on the Word of God just as a carpenter focuses on a nail while hammering it. If the carpenter is not paying attention to what he or she is doing, then the carpenter could get hurt. You and I are the same way. If we are not doing things in accordance with God's Word, we can hurt ourselves. "Be ye doers of the word, and not hearers only, deceiving your own selves," says the Lord (James 1:22, KJV). Doing things in accordance with God's Word develops character, which is more important than talent.

The second tool is your holy temple. In the words of Paul, "I beseech you…, by the mercies of God, that ye present your bodies a living sacrifice, holy, acceptable unto God, which is your reasonable service" (Romans 12:1, KJV). Before God could make available greater use of my talents, I had to make some sacrifices. I had to give up some things in my life that did not glorify the Lord.

I used to enjoy a good bottle of wine or champagne with my friends. In fact, I had a fully stocked, temperature-controlled wine cellar in my house. I didn't see anything wrong with an occasional drink, nor to this day do I judge friends who drink. However, God asked me to stop drinking and to get rid of the cellar and its contents. I gave it away to a friend who had been looking for a similar cellar.

God will speak to you and tell you what you need to give up. God will even take away the urge to do those things. And if necessary, God may strip from your life every thing and every person that can hinder the divine purpose for your life.

To avoid the pain of having to be stripped and start over again, diligently use the first tool—the Word of God.

The third tool is your immediate resources. When Moses was afraid to carry out the directive that God had given him, the Lord asked him,

"What's that in your hand?"

"A staff."

"Throw it on the ground." He threw it. It became a snake; Moses jumped back—fast!

GOD said to Moses, "Reach out and grab it by the tail." He reached out and grabbed it—and he was holding his staff again.

—Exodus 4:2-4, The Message

This simple rod later parted the Red Sea and was a critical tool in delivering the Israelites from bondage.

God always blesses us by using things that are the least obvious to us, such as a pen with which to write or draw.

In 2 Kings 4, the substance to create wealth was sitting in the cupboard of a widow who was in debt. Elisha told her to take her olive oil (which represents divine ideas) and pour it into all the resources she could muster. He told her, "There will be plenty of money to support both you and your sons."

Many of us are sitting on gold mines and may not realize it. What divine ideas are collecting dust in the cupboard of your mind?

The A in *talents* stands for "ability." In the parable of the talents, as described in the King James Version of the Bible, God blessed each servant according to his "several ability" (Matthew 25:15). The word *several* is translated from the Greek word *idios*, which means "one's own."[1] I believe that God never gives you more than you can handle. The better you handle it, the more God gives you.

Billionaire Oprah Winfrey obviously is doing some important things right. The creator of a multibillion-dollar enterprise, she needs to focus on what she does best. So she has a cabinet of delegates who also delegate responsibility. She has attorneys, accountants, producers, editors, writers, cooks, trainers, hairstylists, security guards, and much more—all of whom operate in their gifts so that Oprah can operate in hers.

Increase requires that you learn to be resourceful so that you can be about God's business. How well do you delegate responsibility?

---

1. *James Strong,* The Exhaustive Concordance of the Bible *(Nashville: Abindgon, 1890),* "Greek Dictionary of the New Testament," *#2398.*

The A in *talents* also stands for "anointing." The word *anointing* is translated from the Greek word *crisma,* whose root word means "special endowment."[2] Each of us has at least one special gift, something we were made to do. I enjoy speaking before audiences, and I equally enjoy writing. As I plug into God and partner with the Holy Spirit in my work, I find joy.

The L in *talents* stands for "love." When you do what you love, you are doing what you are good at. An anointing is upon your work. Jesus used the word "good" to indicate that something or someone was functioning properly. "Well done, thou good and faithful servant" (Matthew 25:21, KJV). Jesus fully submitted to his purpose, and people said of him, "He has done all things well; He makes even the deaf to hear and the mute to speak" (Mark 7:37, NASB).

What do you feel passionate about doing? Your God-given tools, ability, anointing, and love (T.A.L.) are everything you need to succeed (E.N.T.S.).

Don't get comfortable with just maintaining. God wants us to take some risks. God wants us to stretch and grow. "Make a careful exploration of who you are and the work you have been given, and then sink yourself into that" (Galatians 6:3, The Message).

Tomorrow I will show you how we minimize our opportunities when we're not good stewards of what God has given us.

Acronym to Remember: **T.A.L.E.N.T.S.**
(**T**ools, **A**bility/**A**nointing, **L**ove; **E**verything **N**eeded **T**o **S**ucceed)

Verses to Remember:
"Make a careful exploration of who you are and the work you have been given, and then sink yourself into that" (Galatians 6:3, The Message).

"We are guides into God's most sublime secrets, not security guards posted to protect them. The requirements for a good guide are reliability and accurate knowledge" (1 Corinthians 4:2, The Message).

---

2. *James Strong,* The Exhaustive Concordance of the Bible *(Nashville: Abindgon, 1890),* "*Greek Dictionary of the New Testament,*" *#5548.*

Questions of the Day:
- What are your talents?

- How can you invest your talents?

- How can society benefit?

- How can your family benefit?

- How can you benefit?

- What would happen if you went through life neglecting to fully invest your talents?

DAY 4

M aintenance
I s
N ot
I ncrease

From everyone who has been given much, much will be demanded; and from the one who has been entrusted with much, much more will be asked.

–Luke 12:48, NIV

There was a time in my life when I had more dash than cash. On the outside, I appeared to be prosperous. I had a high income, a beautiful home that was lavishly furnished, an expensive wardrobe, and a new European luxury convertible. I appeared to be prosperous, but in reality I was withering.

I was just maintaining an expensive lifestyle. My spending habits were not allowing me to grow financially. My finances were stagnant. I was what I call today a Mini-Me. I was being less than my potential.

When the market changed for the worse, I was not in a good position, unlike some of my friends who were better stewards with the Lord's money. They were able to buy undervalued stocks that dropped even lower, positioning themselves for growth when things changed.

Because of some unexpected changes in my life, I had to sell all my holdings and take some deep losses. I was in a crisis and needed the money. I faced a painful reality: I had been wasteful with the money God had given me. I promised God, "If you restore me, I will be a much better steward with your money." I was fortunate; God gave me another chance. God does not always give us another chance.

A lot of us are like fig trees. We are only a figure of what we ought to be. We are comfortable maintaining an image, but we are unwilling to do the things that are necessary to become happy, healthy, and whole, as God has made possible.

What does Jesus do when he sees that we are unwilling to do what it takes to grow?

"Early in the morning, as he was on his way back to the city, he was hungry. Seeing a fig tree by the road, he went up to it but found nothing on it except leaves. Then he said to it, 'May you never bear fruit again!' Immediately the tree withered" (Matthew 21:18-19, NIV).

Jesus does not have to curse us as he did the fig tree. In our souls we curse ourselves when we choose to look like we are growing instead of actually positioning ourselves for growth. Obedience to God positions us for growth.

The leaves represent a false covering. Adam and Eve inadvertently removed themselves from God's covering by listening to the voice of the devil instead of obeying the word of God. They were naked and tried to cover themselves with fig leaves to hide the fact that they had stopped growing spiritually, much like we today buy ourselves things to make us feel better. By the time the bill comes, the good feeling is gone, and we feel deeper pain after realizing how much we have spent.

If you are not growing, you will find yourself in a major crisis when the Master returns and asks the same question he asked of Adam and Eve: "What is this you have done?" (Genesis 3:13, NIV).

What is a crisis? Webster defines the word *crisis* as "a time of great danger or trouble, whose outcome decides whether possible bad consequences will follow."

If you have been consistent in your growth in particular areas of your life, namely spiritual, mental, physical, financial, or relational, a hundredfold blessing occurs. This blessing occurs whenever a crisis appears in the area where you are challenged.

What do I mean by a hundredfold blessing?

If you take a test of a hundred questions and get all the questions right, what would be your percentage? One hundred percent. If you take a test of two questions and get both questions right, what would be your percentage? One hundred percent. A hundredfold blessing is the best possible result under any given circumstance.

If a person who is consistent in feeding her soul comes under spiritual attack, she will have greater success than one who only occasionally feeds her soul. The testing would be an indication that a possible harvest was near. The one who fed her soul would yield fruit.

> Blessed is the man
>> who does not walk in the counsel of the wicked
> or stand in the way of sinners
>> or sit in the seat of mockers.
> But his delight is in the law of the LORD,
>> and on his law he meditates day and night.
> He is like a tree planted by the streams of water,
>> which yields its fruit in season
> and whose leaf does not wither.
>> Whatever he does prospers.

—Psalm 1:1-3, NIV

Adam and Eve erred by following the counsel of an ungodly serpent.

If you have been only maintaining, you might not be able to pass a major test. However, if you have been consistently growing, you will be prepared to handle whatever may be thrown at you.

Job was a diligent man. Yet God allowed Satan to test Job in every area of his life. Satan took his family, health, and wealth, and through false accusations of his friends, Satan was even trying to steal his soul. Because Job praised and worshiped God so much, his spirit was strong enough to endure every test.

"I am full of matter, the spirit within me constraineth me" (Job 32:18, KJV). In P.E.A.C.E. (Power Exercised And Christ Exemplified) God worked out the matter. In the end, Job received a doublefold blessing. God will do the same for you.

By diligently feeding your spirit, you position yourself for manifestation in times of temptation. A manifestation is a public demonstration. It became clear to everyone that God was with Job through his hardships. He could not have survived those rough times without God. The Holy Spirit was in the matter, and Job trusted God.

There is promise in your future. However, you will not realize what God has prepared for you if you continue to do just enough to get by. Doing just enough will not prepare you for the test required to take you to the next level.

Acronym to Remember: **M.I.N.I.**
(**M**aintenance **I**s **N**ot **I**ncrease)

Verse to Remember:
"From everyone who has been given much, much will be demanded; and from the one who has been entrusted with much, much more will be asked" (Luke 12:48, NIV).

Questions of the Day:
• In what ways, if any, have you just been maintaining and not growing?

• What has stopped you?

• What action steps will you take to enable growth?

DAY 5

D estiny
I s
A
M atter
O f
N ot
D oubting

All things can be done for the one who believes.

—Mark 9:23, NRSV

Now to him who is able to do immeasurably more than all we ask or imagine, according to his power that is at work within us …

—Ephesians 3:20, NIV

A diamond is the last and highest of God's mineral creations, just as a human being is the last and highest of God's animal creations. We especially value their finished quality and know that natural or uncut gems are not as valuable. Persons are sometimes referred to as "diamonds in the rough."

Yet many of us look outside ourselves in search of wealth and happiness, and we ignore our immediate milieu. In 2 Kings 4 we read,

> The wife of a man from the guild of prophets called out to Elisha, "Your servant my husband is dead. You well know what a good man he was, devoted to God. And now the man to whom he was in debt is on his way to collect by taking my two children as slaves."
>
> Elisha said, "I wonder how I can be of help. Tell me, what do you have in the house?"
>
> —2 Kings 4:1-2, The Message

Elisha asked her a question to find out where her level of thinking was.

24

Her answer revealed that her thinking was in a state of lack. She claimed to have nothing, except a little oil.

As I mentioned earlier, the oil represents divine substance. The woman had a divine idea worth a fortune sitting in the cupboard of her mind and collecting dust. Because it was in her own house (mind), she thought it wasn't worth much. Nevertheless, the man of God met her where she was.

"Here's what you do," said Elisha. "Go up and down the street and borrow jugs and bowls from all your neighbors. And not just a few—all you can get. Then come home and lock the door behind you, you and your sons. Pour oil into each container; when each is full, set it aside."

—2 Kings 4:3-4, The Message

In other words, look around your immediate environment for resources that can help you. Acquire as many resources as you can. Close the door of your house (your mind) and focus on what you have, not on what you don't have, and pour your ideas into each resource.

She did what he said. She locked the door behind her and her sons; as they brought the containers to her, she filled them. When all the jugs and bowls were full, she said to one of her sons, "Another jug, please."

He said, "That's it. There are no more jugs."

Then the oil stopped.

She went and told the story to the man of God. He said, "Go sell the oil and make good on your debts. Live, both you and your sons, on what's left."

—2 Kings 4:5-7, The Message

When her resources ran out, so did her ideas, and she panicked. Had she not given in to fear, the flow of ideas and resources to pour them into would not have stopped. She could have experienced abundance.

Russell Conwell, the founder of Temple University, traveled the country giving his famous "Acres of Diamonds" speech. He told the story of a farmer named Al Hafed, whose aim was to become immensely rich. He sold his farm to go out and look for diamonds that he could sell to earn his fortune. Al Hafed searched around Palestine for diamonds, then wandered into Europe without finding what he was in search of. At last, when his money was gone, Al Hafed cast himself into a tidal wave and was drowned.

After his death, someone unknowingly found acres of diamonds on the property that Al Hafed had relinquished. These diamonds were worth a fortune. The land he left was filled with the diamonds he sought.

"The kingdom of heaven is like treasure hidden in a field. When a man found it, he hid it again, and then in his joy went and sold all he had and bought that field" (Matthew 13:44, NIV).

The happiness, success, and good fortune you are seeking have already been given to you. This is what Jesus was telling us when he said, "The kingdom of God does not come with your careful observation, nor will people say, 'Here it is,' or 'There it is,' because the kingdom of God is within you" (Luke 17:20-21, NIV).

The kingdom inside you is God's dwelling place. If you are looking for happiness and success outside of God, you won't find it. However, if you look inside of you, as you live a life of praise, you will find everything you are looking for and more. God inhabits the praises of God's people. As I mentioned earlier, *praise* means to "set a price on." You are to set a high value on what God has placed inside you.

Spiritually speaking, land represents the mind. In Russell Conwell's story, Al Hafed sold the land (mind) that God had given him and went in search of his fortune. How many uniquely gifted people choose to look outside their God-given callings or vocations to find their place in this world? How many, after a few major disappointments, place their dreams in the cupboards of their minds and forget about them?

When we don't believe in the gifts and ideas that God has placed inside us, we step outside our callings to find success. I can tell you from previous experience that even if you do find success outside your calling, you won't *feel* successful. Also, your work will not bring glory to God; it is not what the Lord made you to do.

Believe in the gifts that God has given you. Glorify God by using your gifts and following through on the ideas in your mind.

How do you find your calling? God never calls anyone who isn't actively doing something. So do something that is in accordance with your interests and gifting. Each one of the disciples whom Jesus chose was busy in some other occupation. Matthew was a tax collector, Luke was a physician, and many of the other disciples were fishermen.

Prior to becoming a professional speaker, my mentor Les Brown was a radio DJ. On air, he addressed community conditions that needed to be brought into public view. As he mentioned in his book *Up Thoughts in Down Times,* he lost his job as a broadcaster, but the airwaves were not his only platform. God was calling him higher. While serving as a representative in the Ohio legislature, he was invited to speak to a national organization in New Orleans. While receiving a lengthy standing ovation, he knew public speaking was the direction in which God was leading him.

The gift of public speaking, like the kingdom of heaven, was in Les all along. When he found it, he gave up everything and followed his calling. By allowing God to direct him, Les Brown has become one of the highest-paid and most sought-after speakers in the United States.

Believe in your gifts and use them. Look inside for direction and look outside and around you for opportunities. Tomorrow I will share with you how to begin going inside and connecting with the Power Source, J.E.S.U.S. C.H.R.I.S.T. (Jesus' Example Shows Ultimate Surrender/Sacrifice; Courageous Honesty Reaching Inside Spirit/Self & Trusting).

Acronym to Remember: D.I.A.M.O.N.D.
(Destiny Is A Matter Of Not Doubting)

Verse to Remember:
"All things can be done for the one who believes" (Mark 9:23, NRSV).

Questions of the Day:
• What are your diamonds?

- Where are your diamonds?

- What diamonds have you lost?

- Where is the kingdom of God?

- How do you glorify God?

- What did you learn from today's reading, and with whom can you share it?

DAY 6

J esus'
E xample
S hows
U ltimate
S urrender/Sacrifice

C ourageous
H onesty
R eaching
I nside
S pirit/Self &
T rusting

Through the Spirit, Christ offered himself as an unblemished sacrifice, freeing us from all those dead-end efforts to make ourselves respectable, so that we can live all out for God.

—Hebrews 9:11, The Message

Realizing the Christ within you is a matter of surrender. You must let go of your will and practice the presence of God. As John said, "He must increase, but I must decrease" (John 3:30, KJV). God dwells in you to the extent that God's Word lives in you.

Jesus is the Word. To demonstrate his full potential, he frequently had to reach inside himself to connect with God in him. Like us, Jesus "was made in the likeness of men" and was "found in fashion as a man" (Philippians 2:7-8, KJV). He came in such form to show us who we are and what we are capable of doing when we reach inside ourselves and trust the One who lives in us.

Jesus performed numerous miracles. He walked on water, turned water into wine, healed the sick, raised the dead, and even pulled money out of a fish to pay his and the disciples' taxes. He said, "I tell you the truth, anyone who has faith in me will do what I have been doing. He will do even greater things than these" (John 14:12, NIV).

If you are born again, Jesus is inside of you. "Greater is he that is in you, than he that is in the world" (1 John 4:4, KJV). You would never realize this if you neglected to go inside yourself and connect with the One who lives inside you.

Jesus knew that he needed the Father. He often practiced the presence of God. "Anyone who has seen me has seen the Father" (John 14:9, NIV). Jesus' character was a mirror image of the Father's. God is righteous, and like the Father, Jesus is righteous. In the New Testament the word "righteous" translates the Greek root *dikaiosune,* which means "equity of character."[1] Jesus' character is equal to God's.

We are commanded, "Let this mind be in you, which was also in Christ Jesus: who being in the form of God, thought it not robbery to be equal with God" (Philippians 2:5-6, KJV). As Jesus conformed to God, so you and I are to conform to Jesus. "Be not conformed to this world: but be ye transformed by the renewing of your mind" (Romans 12:2, KJV).

It takes great courage to conform to the mind of Christ instead of to the world. You are influenced by the One within you, the C.H.R.I.S.T. (Courageous Honesty; Reaching Inside Self & Trusting), while others, without even thinking, are influenced by the culture. It's a different way of living than what most of us are accustomed to.

Realizing your Christlikeness requires that you let go of all attitudes and behaviors that are ungodly, relinquishing all of your F.A.L.S.E. G.O.D.S. (Fear/Fornication, Anger/Adultery, Lust/Lasciviousness, Sloth, Envy, Greed, Overindulgence, Despair, Stupidity/Sin). Sin will keep you out of your full potential and out of the kingdom within. "You shall have no other gods before me" (Exodus 20:3, NIV). You cannot enter the presence of God when you put anything else before God; this includes yourself and your personal desires.

---

1. *James Strong.* The Exhaustive Concordance of the Bible *(Nashville: Abingdon, 1890),* "*Greek Dictionary in the New Testament,*" *#1342.*

J.E.S.U.S. (Jesus' Example Shows Ultimate Surrender) put God before everything. He could have chosen to get caught up in lust, but he didn't. Luke 4:1-13 tells us how Jesus was tempted to use his personal power to fulfill desires of the flesh. He refused. "My food," said Jesus, "is to do the will of him that sent me and to finish his work" (John 4:34, NIV).

He could have had material success in abundance, but he didn't focus on material gain. He said, "I have come down from heaven, not to do My own will, but the will of Him who sent Me" (John 6:38, NASB).

I am by no means advocating that one should not enjoy abundant living. After all, that's what Jesus came to provide. "I came that you might have life and have it more abundantly" (John 10:10, paraphrase). However, I want you to understand that abundant living is a natural byproduct of surrendering your mind completely to God and doing what the Lord placed you on this earth to do. Putting anything before God is making those things or people your god. Jesus said: "Worship the Lord your God, and serve only him" (Luke 4:8, NRSV).

Ralph Waldo Emerson understood this when he said, "What will you have? quoth God; pay for it and take it."[2] The price for everything that you desire is righteousness, having equal character with Christ. It is paid for by surrendering your will and following his directives. "Seek (aim at and strive after) first of all His kingdom and His righteousness (His way of doing and being right), and then all these things taken together will be given you besides" (Matthew 6:33, Amplified New Testament).

Acronym to Remember: **J.E.S.U.S. C.H.R.I.S.T.**
(**J**esus' **E**xample **S**hows **U**ltimate **S**urrender;
Courageous **H**onesty **R**eaching **I**nside **S**elf & **T**rusting)

Verse to Remember:
"Through the Spirit, Christ offered himself as an unblemished sacrifice, freeing us from all those dead-end efforts to make ourselves respectable,

---

2. *Ralph Waldo Emerson. From "Compensation," in* Emerson's Essays, 79. *Copyright 1926 by Thomas Y. Crowell Company, Inc. Permission to reprint granted by Harper-Collins Publishers.*

so that we can live all out for God" (Hebrews 9:11, The Message).

Questions of the Day:
• What must you do to practice the presence of God?

• To what extent does God dwell in us?

• Why do you think Jesus came to earth in human form?

• What does righteousness mean?

• How do you conform your mind to the mind of Christ?

• How surrendered to God are you?

DAY 7

A
F aithful
F riend
I s
R eminding
M e

If you love me, show it by doing what I've told you. I will talk to the Father, and he'll provide you another Friend so that you will always have someone with you. This Friend is the Spirit of Truth.

—John 14:15-16, The Message

When asked who we are, we answer this question on the level at which we think. People who think shallow can only give shallow answers, such as "I'm Ed Gray. I'm a Christian. I'm an African American. I'm a speaker and writer." There is a lot more to you than your name, religion, race, occupation, and past.

Our answers are shallow because we rarely think deeply about the W.A.Y. (Who Are You?) in Christ. Jesus said, "I am the way" (John 14:6, NIV). Jesus is the path to God. To discover the truth about your identity, you must go beneath the surface and tap into Jesus.

Who am I? "I have called you friends, for everything that I learned from my Father I have made known to you. You did not choose me, but I chose you and appointed you and appointed you to bear fruit—fruit that will last" (John 15:15-16, NIV). Wow! I am a friend of Jesus, and so are you, if we keep his commands (John 15:14).

"Yet to all who received him, to those who believed in his name, he gave the right to become children of God—children born not of natural descent, nor of human decision or a husband's will, but born of God" (John 1:12-13, NIV). We are children of God. We affirm that we are God's children by being led by the Spirit.

"For as many as are led by the Spirit of God, they are the sons of God" (Romans 8:14, KJV). The Spirit can lead you to do and say the right things, even though you want to do the wrong things. For example, you might know, from your last physical exam, that you are unhealthy. Your doctor might have told you that you have high cholesterol or high blood pressure. She told you to diet and exercise, but you really don't want to, as you have gotten used to an unhealthy lifestyle. Exercise is work, and eating right is not always easy.

A quiet voice—your Friend whom God has sent—tells you, "Don't order those fried lemon-pepper chicken wings; they will raise your cholesterol."

Your mind says, "They taste good."

You lie to yourself and the Christ who is within you and say, "I'll eat only a few and I'll start eating right tomorrow."

Your disobedience affirms that you are not led by the Spirit but by the flesh. You'd rather eat the flesh of a fried chicken and make yourself sick than obey the voice of God. Your response to the Spirit of God, who is always speaking to you, reveals whether or not you are truly a child of God. Sons and daughters of God obey God's voice and have fruit to show for it.

Daniel was a son of God. He had the opportunity to order food that was fit for a king on a daily basis. Instead Daniel and his two companions chose to glorify God. They ate simple foods and foods that were not involved in pagan religious practices. "Daniel resolved not to defile himself with the royal food and wine, and he asked the chief official for permission not to defile himself this way" (Daniel 1:8, NIV). We have to resolve to do the same thing physically, mentally, and spiritually.

A.F.F.I.R.M. (A Faithful Friend Is Reminding Me), "Don't you know that you yourselves are God's temple and that God's Spirit lives in you? If anyone destroys God's temple, God will destroy him; for God's temple is sacred, and you are that temple" (1 Corinthians 3:16-17, NIV). God allows us to destroy ourselves. All we have to do is neglect our bodies, and our health begins to deteriorate.

> God created man in his own image,
> in the image of God he created him;
> male and female he created them.
>
> —Genesis 1:27, NIV

When we think less of ourselves than we should, we suffer from what psychologists call "low self-esteem." Low self-esteem is simply placing a veil over your soul and covering up the powerful person you are in Christ.

There is no need to have low self-esteem or to feel guilt or shame. When Jesus paid the price on the cross for our sins, the veil that separated us from God was removed. This meant that direct access to God was once again available. "Since we were restored to friendship with God by the death of his Son while we were still his enemies, we will certainly be delivered from eternal punishment by his life" (Romans 5:10, NLT). This requires that we live lives that reflect Christ; otherwise, we have chosen to separate ourselves from God in spite of what Christ has done to make it possible.

If you have placed the veil on, take it off so that you can begin to reflect more of God. "We, who with unveiled faces all reflect the Lord's glory, are being transformed into his likeness with ever-increasing glory, which comes from the Lord, who is Spirit" (2 Corinthians 3:18, NIV). We are to be reflections of God in every area of our lives: spiritual, mental, physical, financial, and relational.

When my self-esteem is low and I attack those who produce godlike fruits, God reminds me, "All of you are children of the Most High" (Psalm 82:6, NKJV).

When we are not producing results, it is usually because of disobedience to God. Disobedience is equivalent to disbelief.

A.F.F.I.R.M. (A Faithful Friend Is Reminding Me) to live up to my divine potential. "From everyone who has been given much, much shall be required; and to whom they entrusted much, of him they will ask all the more" (Luke 12:48, NASB). I am reminded that my responsibilities don't get easier; they just get bigger. I have unlimited potential. "I can do all things through Him who strengthens me" (Philippians 4:13, NASB).

A.F.F.I.R.M. (A Faithful Friend Is Reminding Me). "With man this is impossible, but with God all things are possible" (Matthew 19:26, NIV). God reminds me that I need God.

Just as Jesus affirms me, so I am to affirm others. He said, "A new command I give you: Love one another. As I have loved you, so must you love one another. By this all men will know that you are my disciples, if you love one another" (John 13:34-35, NIV).

Disciple comes from the word *discipline,* which means "instruction and exercise designed to train to proper conduct and action." We are to disciple one another by affirming one another.

Webster defines *affirm* as "to state or assert positively; maintain as true." As a disciple, I am to remind you that you are good and that you are a child of God when you forget. Because I love you, I am to assist you when I see that you need help. I am not to do the work for you, but I am to teach you how to do the work yourself, just as Jesus has shown me. By affirming one another, we make ourselves firm in Christ. We demonstrate that we are indeed friends of God.

Acronym to Remember: A.F.F.I.R.M.
(A Faithful Friend Is Reminding Me)

Verse to Remember:
"I have called you friends, for everything that I learned from my Father I have made known to you. You did not choose me, but I chose you and appointed you to bear fruit—fruit that will last" (John 15:15-16, NIV).

Questions of the Day:
• What are you to Christ?

• How do you gain the right to become a child of God?

- What does the Spirit of God lead you to do?

- Describe the last time you allowed yourself to be led by the Spirit.

- How did you feel afterward?

- What does disobedience to the Spirit affirm?

- What are some things you can do to affirm others?

Confidence
to move beyond
limitations

DAY 8

C ancel
O ut
N egativity;
F aith
I s
D ivine
E mpowerment &
N ecessary
C hrist
E nlightenment

I can do all things through Christ who strengthens me.

–Philippians 4:13, NKJV

Octavia Butler, one of the the grand dames of science fiction writers, once told her aunt that she wanted to be a writer. Her aunt replied, "Honey, Negroes can't be writers." Fortunately, Octavia listened to the voice of God that was inside her instead of the inhibiting voices that were trying to creep in and stop her from becoming who and what she was meant to be.

Satan will use others to carry out his desire to rob you of your destiny. The people he uses often have no idea that their words are being used to kill your hopes and dreams. Many of them have allowed Satan to rob them of their own dreams. Because they think the realization of a dream is impossible for them, they believe it is also impossible for you. As a result of their giving into negative subtleties, Satan controls their minds and binds their dreams. He uses them as agents to rob others. Jesus said of such people, "You belong to your father, the devil, and you want to carry out your father's desire" (John 8:44, NIV).

Satan is a thief. He "comes only to steal and kill and destroy" (John 10:10, NIV). When I was a child, my destiny was almost stolen from me. In the first grade I was wrongfully labeled a slow learner. I believed it to be true and failed first grade. For me to begin walking in my destiny, the label placed on me as a child had to be peeled off. I had to cancel the negative, limiting way that I saw myself.

The cost that needed to be paid for you and me to become all that we can be has already been paid at the cross. To realize this truth, we must pick up the cross daily. The cross is not our cross but Christ's cross. As Paul realized, "I have been crucified with Christ and I no longer live, but Christ lives in me. The life I live in the body, I live by faith in the Son of God, who loved me and gave himself for me" (Galatians 2:20, NIV).

The realization of who you are in Christ provides a powerful frame of reference. It gives you insight into what you are capable of accomplishing by working in concert with Christ. In one letter Paul tells us, "I can do all things through Christ who strengthens me" (Philippians 4:13, NKJV). Now, this doesn't mean that I can get on the golf course and beat Tiger Woods. Golf is not my calling.

I believe my purpose is to educate. *Educate* means to "draw out of." I am called to draw out of others the power of God that is within them and to inspire them to carry out their purpose for being on this earth. I accomplish my work through delivering speeches and lectures as well as writing articles and books such as this. Through Christ, I believe I am the best in the world at what I do. Is that cocky? No! It is C.O.N.F.I.D.E.N.C.E. (Cancel Out Negativity; Faith Is Divine Empowerment & Necessary Christ Enlightenment), which is God-confidence. It comes as a result of knowing who you are in Christ and operating in Christ.

Cockiness is self-confidence, thinking that it is you who is doing the work and making things happen. The Bible says, "Don't be so naive and self-confident. You're not exempt. You could fall flat on your face as easily as anyone else. Forget about self-confidence; it's useless. Cultivate God-confidence" (1 Corinthians 10:11, The Message). People who are cocky increase themselves. Their E.G.O.s Edge God Out. People with C.O.N.F.I.D.E.N.C.E., on the other hand, radiate the love of Christ that makes them irresistible magnets, drawing people and opportunities their way. Those who are unaware that this magnetic power is available to all refer to people who have it as lucky. It's not luck; it's C.O.N.F.I.D.E.N.C.E.

Because many of us don't know who we are in Christ, "we live lives of quiet desperation," as Henry David Thoreau put it. But the Bible gives us this divine assurance:

> He gives strength to the weary
> and increases the power of the weak. . . .
> They will soar on wings like eagles.
>
> —Isaiah 40:29,31, NIV

Still, we say to ourselves, "I want to soar on wings like an eagle, but I don't believe I can fly. I am just a humble servant; I don't believe I can do great things."

Wake up! Regardless of what God has called you to do, you are more than capable of doing it, and doing it exceedingly well. It is not you who is doing the work but Christ within you who is doing it. All you have to do is get started. The Lord will lead and guide you. Accepting less than what you are capable of doing and remaining at that level is false humility.

Jesus said, "I tell you the truth, anyone who has faith in me will do what I have been doing. He will do even greater things than these" (John 14:12, NIV).

The Son brings glory to the Father when you and I walk in faith. Whenever someone tells you that you can't do something God is leading you to do, don't argue with him or her, but rebuke that negative thought in the Spirit. Quote to yourself, "I can do all things through Christ who strengthens me." Don't just recite this Scripture; act upon it. Reward yourself. Put a quarter in a piggy bank every time you take action against voices that say, "You can't" or "It's impossible."

Years ago, some people told me that I couldn't get a column in the ninth-largest paper in the U. S. They said, "That's reserved for established journalists who have paid their dues. You don't have any journalism experience." Through Christ, that vision was accomplished, and more. My articles were published in the *Detroit News*, as well as other newspapers, for over nine years, until I stopped writing them to focus on writing books.

In 1987 a friend said, "You can't be a motivational speaker. How many black speakers do you see?" By not listening to that voice and pressing forward, I discovered that all things are possible for those who believe. When someone tells you, "You can't," or when you yourself think, *I can't,* let the light of the Word of God remove the darkness by speaking to yourself God's reaffirming word. Let the Word of God move in power by immediately taking some sort of action toward the dream or desire that is calling you.

If you want to start your own business, your action can be as simple as going to the Small Business Administration in your area and finding out how to get started or working on a business plan. From your small actions, God begins to do the rest.

Early in my speaking career, I had a dream of filling up a large ballroom at the Westin Hotel in downtown Detroit. In my meditation the voice of God said, "Call the Westin Hotel."

I asked myself, *Why?* I began to think about my dream of filling the ballroom. A negative thought entered my mind: *You can't afford the Westin!* At that time, I could not afford the Westin, but God could. I thought about something I had told others: "Even if you can't afford something, the least you can do is to find out how much it will cost and ask God to provide." I took my own advice.

I called and asked for Catering and Sales. A young lady answered the phone in the sales department. She said, "This is Shawna." I introduced myself and told her what I wanted.

She asked the date when I was planning the event. I threw out a date that was eight weeks out. She answered, "For anyone else, that would cost fifteen hundred dollars, but for you, Ed Gray—one hundred dollars."

I thought she was joking. I said, "What?"

She said, "A hundred dollars, but you'll have to pay the taxes."

She explained that we had volunteered together on a planning committee for the NAACP. She felt led to help me. Had I not resisted the negative voice outside me and not responded to the voice of God inside me, I would have missed the blessing that God had set up for me.

From that one action a chain of positive events took place. Karen Dumas, a well-known publicist in Detroit, volunteered to work with me. That event, and subsequent events, got major radio, television, and print exposure. It was the impetus for a lot of other things that occurred, such as my getting into local radio and television, which was a set-up for national radio syndication and a newspaper column.

Shut the devil up by acting upon the voice of God, who is telling you that all things are possible. Reward yourself for shutting up the devil. Remember to put a quarter in a piggy bank every time you take action against voices that say, "you can't," or "it's impossible." By the time the bank is full, you will know that you can indeed do all things through Christ who strengthens you. Reward yourself with a gift or a sentimental reminder of what can be accomplished through C.O.N.F.I.D.E.N.C.E. I prefer to reward the bank's contents to someone else who needs encouragement after sharing my testimony with them. However God leads you, follow in C.O.N.F.I.D.E.N.C.E.

Acronym to Remember: **C.O.N.F.I.D.E.N.C.E.**
(**C**ancel **O**ut **N**egativity; **F**aith **I**s **D**ivine **E**mpowerment
& **N**ecessary **C**hrist **E**nlightenment)

Verse to Remember:
"I can do all things through Christ who strengthens me" (Philippians 4:13, NKJV).

Questions of the Day:
- Describe a time in your life when you allowed a negative thought to talk you out of pursuing a dream or goal.

- Describe a time when you felt God was talking to you and you obeyed.

- What is the difference between cockiness and confidence?

- What is Satan's purpose?

- Read Genesis 3 and in your own words describe how Satan tries to trick us.

- What can you do to prevent Satan from robbing you of your destiny?

- What can you accomplish through Christ, and why?

DAY 9

A ctively
R aise
I deas &
S ubstantiate
E vidence

I will exalt you, O LORD,
>	for you lifted me out of the depths
>	and did not let my enemies gloat over me.
O LORD my God, I called to you for help
>	and you healed me.

—Psalm 30:1-2, NIV

When Jesus healed, he often instructed the recipient to arise. The word *arise* is translated from the Greek word *egeiro,* whose root word means "awake."[1] We have to wake up and move forward in faith.

You can ask Jesus to heal you. If you believe that he is able, he will indeed heal you, according to his will. The healing does not always occur in the physical realm. However, he will give you the emotional resolve to get through your ordeal. He demonstrated this same resolve when he himself endured pain and death on Calvary. He could have saved himself. However, there was a divine purpose for his suffering. After his death, he arose so that all who believe would have life.

If the molecular character of your faith is weak, your prayer requests cannot be advanced to the healing stage. "According to your faith be it unto you" (Matthew 9:29, KJV). Grasping this phenomenon requires an understanding of faith.

---

1. *James Strong,* The Exhaustive Concordance of the Bible *(Nashville: Abingdon, 1890),* "Greek Dictionary of the New Testament," *#1453.*

"Now faith is the substance of things hoped for, the evidence of things not seen" (Hebrews 11:1, KJV). The word *substance* is two words put together. *Sub* means "under" or "below." The word *stance* means "position" or "condition."

Healing may not occur if the condition of your faith is sub par, or below God's acceptable standard. I am not implying that you have to feel right in order for miracles to occur. Faith is not about feelings. It's a mental position of belief in spite of what things may look like. The level at which miracles occur is below your conscious understanding. Therefore, it is not for you to understand how it's going to happen. Again, it is subconscious, below your feeling or knowledge.

Webster defines *conscious* as "having a feeling or knowledge." Your subconscious is the mind of Christ that is within you. "Greater is he that is in you, than he that is in the world" (1 John 4:4, KJV). His residence within you is much deeper than your feelings.

"But we have the mind of Christ" (1 Corinthians 2:16, KJV). This includes you! Jesus is in your Subconscious Mind. At this moment, he's doing trillions of things on your behalf, all of which you are unaware of. You are unaware that he is regulating the flow of blood in your body, fighting germs, and making sure enough oxygen gets to your heart. Many of these things you don't even feel as they occur. He does these things effortlessly for you and without your even asking, even as you sleep. The more Christ substance you have in you, the more power you have to demonstrate his power in ways other than just miraculous bodily functions.

Faith is something that you have to work on regularly to develop fully. As you continue adding the characteristics of Christ, you strengthen the character of your faith. You will eventually rise above the problems and cares of this world and into the realm of the supernatural, even though you are in this world (John 14:1-3).

The evidence is proof. "You will know them by their fruits" (Matthew 7:16, NASB). Jesus said, "Believe me when I say that I am in the Father and the Father is in me; or at least believe on the evidence of the miracles themselves" (John 14:11, NIV).

The ecological system of all God's creations works in the same manner. For example, seeds with the character or structure of apple trees produce apples. Seeds with the structure of orange trees produce oranges. Likewise, those of us who are in Christ, and who develop the character of God in Christ, can produce like Christ. "I tell you the truth, anyone who has faith in me will do what I have been doing. He will do even greater things than these, because I am going to the Father" (John 14:12, NIV). Jesus goes to God on our behalf.

The realization of this power is a progressive realization, one step at a time. It requires that you continue adding characteristics of Christ to your faith. It is part of the work that you must do to "work out your own salvation" (Philippians 2:12, KJV).

The apostles came up and said to the Master, "Give us more faith."

But the Master said, "You don't need *more* faith. There is no 'more' or 'less' in faith. If you have a bare kernel of faith, say the size of a poppy seed, you could say to this sycamore tree, 'Go jump in the lake,' and it would do it."

—Luke 17:5-6, The Message

God has given us the power to do great things through faith. However, it is our responsibility to develop our faith. "According to your faith be it unto you" (Matthew 9:29, KJV).

"Giving all diligence, add to your faith virtue; and to virtue knowledge; and to knowledge temperance; and to temperance patience; and to patience godliness; and to godliness brotherly kindness; and to brotherly kindness charity" (2 Peter 1:5-6, KJV). *Charity* is another word for love.

It is your faith that makes you whole. A lover doesn't make you whole, nor do family or friends. It's not a job that makes you whole, nor is it money. It's faith. After Jesus healed people, he frequently told them, "Arise. Your faith has made you whole."

To lack any of the character traits of Jesus in your faith is to be incomplete. This is why it is important to diligently add to your faith. It's a lifetime journey. The sooner you start adding to your faith, the further along you get.

Love is the most important character trait. Paul understood this when he said, "No matter what I say, what I believe, and what I do, I'm bankrupt without love" (1 Corinthians 13:3, The Message). Love is achieved through godliness, because godliness glorifies God. When you glorify God, you walk in divine glory and realize the purity of divine love.

It is the fear of being alone and without God's protection that allows more fear to enter your life. Fear is the opposite of love. Fear is the opposite of God. Fear is a demonic force that we sometimes allow to enter our minds. It pervades our spirits and affects other areas of our lives, such as the mind, body, finances, and relationships. Glorifying God helps you to realize God's pure love. "There is no fear in love; but perfect love casts out fear, because fear involves torment" (1 John 4:18, NKJV).

A good example of this is found in Luke.

> As [Jesus] was going into a village, ten men who had leprosy met him. They stood at a distance and called out in a loud voice, "Jesus, Master, have pity on us!"
>
> When he saw them, he said, "Go show yourselves to the priests." And as they went they were cleansed.
>
> One of them, when he saw he was healed, came back, praising God in a loud voice. He threw himself at Jesus' feet and thanked him—and he was a Samaritan.
>
> Jesus asked, "Were not all ten cleansed? Where are the other nine? Was no one found to return and give praise to God except this foreigner?" Then he said to him, "Rise and go; your faith has made you well."
>
> —Luke 17:11-19, NIV

In the King James Version that last statement reads, "Thy faith hath made thee whole" (Luke 17:19). The one leper who was healed represents completed faith.

There is a big difference between cleansing and healing. The word *cleanse,* in its Greek form, *katharizo,* means "to be purified."[2] The nine were cleansed, but only one was healed.

The nine lepers had incomplete faith. It appears the desire for godliness was not part of their faith. Because of this, they did not glorify the Lord.

To be healed means to be made perfectly whole. Referring to Jesus and foretelling how our healing would come, Isaiah wrote,

---

2. *James Strong,* The Exhaustive Concordance of the Bible *(Nashville: Abingdon, 1890),* "Greek Dictionary of the New Testament," *#2511.*

He was looked down on and passed over,
    a man who suffered, who knew pain firsthand.
One look at him and people turned away.
    We looked down on him, thought he was scum.
But the fact is, it was *our* pains he carried—
    our disfigurements, and all the things wrong with us.
We thought he brought it on himself,
    that God was punishing him for his own failures.
But it was our sins that did that to him,
    that ripped and tore and crushed him—our sins!
He took the punishment, and that made us whole.
    Through his bruises we get healed.

—Isaiah 53:5-11, The Message

When Christ died at Calvary, provisions were made for your well-being. However, you must accept his gift and choose to arise. As I explained earlier, arise means "to awake." Through faith we must awake to the miracles that are being performed in our lives.

Jesus has already healed your finances. He has already healed your broken heart. He knows what you and I are in need of before we even ask. However, we will not come into the full realization of our healing unless our faith includes virtue, knowledge, self-control, patience, brotherly kindness, and most importantly, love, which is achieved through godliness.

Godliness raises ideas. The one leper who was healed thought about God's goodness, and it brought him to his knees. Think about all that you have to be thankful for. Take some moments to pause and reflect. A realization of how good God is and how merciful God has been to you provides you with a key to heaven.

I admire the humility of music legend Eric Clapton, and I enjoy his music. Clapton experienced a lot of misfortune in life. His mother abandoned him, and his grandparents raised him. His four-year-old son died tragically many years ago. He has done some things of which he is not proud: he had a drug addiction, stole someone's wife, cheated on her, and fathered a child out of wedlock. As a result, his wife divorced him.

In a song in remembrance of his son, he wrote, "I know I don't belong here in heaven." It is that kind of humility that will get you into heaven! Why? It reminds you that you need God's grace. "Blessed are the poor in spirit: for theirs is the kingdom of heaven" (Matthew 5:3, KJV). "For it is by grace you have been saved, through faith—and this not from yourselves, it is the gift of God—not by works, so that no one can boast" (Ephesians 2:8-9, NIV).

Godliness does not mean that you are perfect, for no one is perfect but God. Godliness means that you are willing to make things right, especially in your faith. Whatever has happened in your life, God can restore you if you raise ideas and look for ways to make things right.

> Jesus told his disciples: "There was a rich man whose manager was accused of wasting his possessions. So he called him in and asked him, 'What is this I hear about you? Give an account of your management, because you cannot manage any longer.'"
>
> —Luke 16:1-2, NIV

Raising ideas starts with an open-ended question of possibilities and an honest personal assessment of your values, strengths, and weaknesses. Jesus' story goes on:

> The manager said to himself, "What shall I do now? My master is taking away my job. I'm not strong enough to dig, and I'm ashamed to beg—I know what I'll do so that, when I lose my job here, people will welcome me into their houses."
>
> So he called each one of his master's debtors. He asked the first, "How much do you owe my master?"
>
> "Eight hundred gallons of olive oil," he replied.
>
> The manager told him, "Take your bill, sit down quickly, and make it four hundred."
>
> Then he asked the second, "And how much do you owe?"
>
> "A thousand bushels of wheat," he replied.
>
> He told him, "Take your bill and make it eight hundred."
>
> The master commended the dishonest manager because he acted shrewdly. For the people of this world are more shrewd in dealing with their own kind than the people of the light.
>
> —Luke 16:3-8, NIV

Make your friends before you need them. The best friend you can have is Jesus. Worship brings you into intimate relationship with him. You also need people.

Looking back at the leper who was cleansed and healed, it is evident that he had some type of demon in his life. This we know because Jesus cleansed him.

Like the leper, the shrewd manager had a foul spirit. He had been stealing. However, he used his faith to rise out of the situation. To stay out of trouble, the shrewd steward had to continuously work on his faith, especially his godliness. The fact that he began to think outside the box, and because his master commended his efforts, suggests that he had already awakened to this idea.

It is unfortunate, but so-called worldly people demonstrate greater faith than do so-called Christians. People raising ideas, and substantiating the evidence of those ideas by taking risks, create fortunes. Being a Christian is not a subscription to a quiet life of desperation. Being a Christian is a subscription to manifesting the characteristics and glory of God in our lives by adding to our faith. We are more capable of succeeding than anyone else, if we just choose to arise.

God has given you the power to get well. "Remember the LORD your God, for it is he who gives you the ability to produce wealth, and so confirms the covenant, which he swore to your forefathers, as it is today" (Deuteronomy 8:18, NIV). One of our forefathers whom God made rich was a man named Abraham.

"Wasn't our ancestor Abraham 'made right with God' by works when he placed his son Isaac on the sacrificial altar? Isn't it obvious that faith and works are yoked partners, that faith expresses itself in works?" (James 2:21, The Message). Continuously adding to your faith is the way to create a life of G.O.L.D. (God-Ordained Life Development).

Acronym to Remember: **A.R.I.S.E.**
(**A**ctively **R**aise **I**deas & **S**ubstantiate **E**vidence)

Verse to Remember:
"According to your faith be it unto you" (Matthew 9:29, KJV).

Questions of the Day:
- Look at Hebrews 11:1 and in your own words define *faith*.

- Look at Matthew 9:29 and describe the importance of faith.

- Describe the role of faith in healing.

- What is the difference between cleansing and healing?

- What's required to be healed?

- At present, how is your faith?

DAY 10

G od-
O rdained
L ife
D evelopment

We are his workmanship, created in Christ Jesus unto good works, which God hath before ordained that we should walk in them.

–Ephesians 2:10, KJV

The Almighty will be your gold,
the choicest silver for you.

–Job 22:25, NIV

Gold is soft and brittle in its purest form. By itself, it is not usable. Strengthening gold requires work. Therefore, it is melted down, other metals are added, and then it is shaped and formed.

Faith is like gold. Alone, it is too malleable to be of full use. "Even so faith, if it has no works, is dead, being by itself" (James 2:17, NASB).

To strengthen our faith so that it is usable requires additional work. "Giving all diligence, add to your faith virtue; and to virtue knowledge; and to knowledge temperance; and to temperance patience; and to patience godliness; and to godliness brotherly kindness; and to brotherly kindness charity" (2 Peter 1:5-6, KJV).

Paul said, "Forgetting what is behind and straining toward what is ahead, I press on toward the goal to win the prize for which God has called me heavenward in Christ Jesus" (Philippians 3:13-14, NIV). Early in his ministry, Paul possessed faith, but he lacked virtue, self-control, patience, godliness, and brotherly kindness. This was seen in his blame-game confrontation with Peter. Paul said, "Now when Peter had come to Antioch, I withstood him to the face, because he was to be blamed" (Galatians 2:11, NKJV).

If Paul disliked someone, he didn't restrain his feelings. Early on, it appeared that he disliked Mark and did not want Mark traveling with him. However, Paul later humbled himself and wrote to Timothy, "Get Mark and bring him with you, for he is useful to me for ministry" (2 Timothy 4:11, NKJV). As Paul added virtue, self-control, patience, godliness, and brotherly kindness to his faith, he matured and grew even stronger in his faith. Paul was able to press on, in spite of his many adversities, because he allowed the Holy Spirit to take over his thoughts and actions.

Faith differs from gold in that its refinement is constant. On a daily basis you must add virtue. Virtue is added by conforming your life and conduct to the Christ-Mind, thinking, acting, and living in accordance with holy ways.

On a daily basis we are to add knowledge to our virtue. Knowledge is added by constantly entering God's classroom, through prayer and meditation and receiving spiritual knowledge (1 Corinthians 2:16). I pray and meditate at appointed times daily. Every morning I meditate and pray. I meditate and pray again in the evening, after I have completed my workday.

The words I am sharing with you in this book are the byproducts of the time I've spent receiving knowledge in God's classroom. It is a spiritual Ph.D. (Persistent Higher Development) program that only those who are seeking the face of God can enter. Although it is a prerequisite to grow, it is offered as an elective course.

"Without faith it is impossible to please him: for he that cometh to God must believe that he is, and that he is a rewarder of them that diligently seek him" (Hebrews 11:6, KJV). This may require that you wake up earlier in the morning to meet with God, if you don't seem to have time to seek God diligently.

Knowledge is added to your virtue by spending time daily in personal study. This is not just study of the Bible but gaining more knowledge of what's going on in your industry or profession, studying science, the arts, and literature, and keeping up with current affairs. In Daniel's day, those who were selected by the king to enter into the "Ph.D. program" were those who showed an aptitude for every kind of learning—well informed, quick to understand, and qualified to serve in the king's palace (Daniel 1:4). Having many frames of reference develops a cogent mind.

The constant acquisition of knowledge will make you more valuable to the people you serve. How comfortable would you feel going to a doctor, accountant, or any other professional who is not abreast of the most current knowledge in his or her given field? How would you feel going to a pastor who lacked life experience and spent little time communing with God? The pastor's limited frames of reference would make it difficult for him or her to meet you where you are and provide divine wisdom.

A friend of mine was amazed at how much professional speakers earn for speaking less than an hour. I explained to him that people don't pay you for your time; they pay you for what you know. You can't put a price on knowledge. However, a lack of knowledge can cost you your life. "My people are destroyed for lack of knowledge" (Hosea 4:6, KJV). Therefore, a person of God who imparts godly wisdom is worthy of his or her hire (Luke 10:7).

We must constantly add self-control to our knowledge. "A wise man holds his tongue. Only a fool blurts out everything he knows; that only leads to sorrow and trouble" (Proverbs 10:14, TLB). Some things must be kept in S.E.C.R.E.T. (Sometimes Even Christ Reserves Enlightening Truths). At times it is important that you withhold what you know until God tells you it is time to reveal it. This requires that you add patience to your self-control.

Great comedians demonstrate excellent timing when telling jokes. They don't rush to the punch line; they wait for the right moment, and their jokes sneak up on you and make you laugh.

Whatever you do, even if it's crossing the street or driving a car, you must be patient and wait for the right time. Many people have caused accidents, and hurt themselves severely, because they were impatient.

To our patience we are to add godliness. The book of Genesis is the story of creation. Order is the first lesson of creation. God has a method to how God does things. Being made in God's image and likeness, we are to "let all things be done decently and in order" (1 Corinthians 14:40, KJV). God doesn't want us to be indecent in our dealings with others or to be hodgepodge in our work. Everything we do should be done in a spirit of excellence.

To our godliness we are to add brotherly kindness and love. "Treat people the same way you want them to treat you" (Matthew 7:12, NASB).

G.O.L.D. (God-Ordained Life Development) requires that you add to your faith and R.E.F.I.N.E. (Repeating Every day; Faith Is Not Enough). Spiritual gold is a progressive realization one day at a time toward a divine finish.

Acronym to Remember: **G.O.L.D.**
(God-Ordained Life Development)

Verse to Remember:
"We are his workmanship, created in Christ Jesus unto good works, which God hath before ordained that we should walk in them" (Ephesians 2:10, KJV).

Questions of the Day:
• What is the present condition of your faith?

• Read 2 Peter 1:5-6 and describe what needs to be added to your faith to make it strong.

• Read Hebrews 11:6 and describe why faith is important.

DAY 11

B oldly
E mbrace
Y our
O wn
N atural
D estiny

L ife
I s
M easured
I n
T hought;
A bundant
T hinking
I s
O f
N ecessity

As he thinks within himself, so he is.

—Proverbs 23:7, NASB

Many people try to place God in a box, limiting the Lord by their own understanding. If I said, "I will do the same works that Jesus did—and even better ones," some people would be frightened and might accuse me of blasphemy. But Christ himself said, "I tell you the truth, anyone who has faith in me will do what I have been doing. He will do even greater things than these" (John 14:12, NIV).

Because of fear, many of us have difficulty accepting the power given to us. As a result, we are unable to move B.E.Y.O.N.D. L.I.M.I.T.A.T.I.O.N.

"God hath not given us the spirit of fear; but of power, and of love, and of a sound mind" (2 Timothy 1:7, KJV). The following are steps for moving beyond limitations:

1. **Look beyond what you see as possible.** Remember, "with God all things are possible" (Matthew 19:26, KJV).

   When I received the vision in 1989 to share my thoughts with people all over the world, I did not know how I would begin. I was not well known or well connected. Over 90 percent of all the people I knew lived in Detroit. Now my thoughts are broadcast throughout the United States.

2. **Write down your vision.** In words from Habakkuk,
   Record the vision
   And inscribe it on tablets,
   That one who reads it may run.
   For the vision is yet for the appointed time;
   It hastens toward the goal, and it will not fail.
   Though it tarries, wait for it;
   For it will certainly come, it will not delay.

   —Habakkuk 2:2-3, NASB

3. **Put your vision on tape, and listen to it twice daily until it happens.** "Faith comes from hearing, and hearing by the word of Christ" (Romans 10:17, NASB). There is power in repetition. By repetitiously hearing something, your subconscious absorbs it. You begin to believe it at deeper levels, and the steps you need to take reveal themselves to you. Subsequently, the resources you need are drawn to you.

4. **Don't share your dreams with dream killers.** Dream killers are often close friends and family members who do not mean you any harm. They simply do not have a lot of faith but rather rely on things they see from their limited frames of reference. God did not give them your vision; God gave it to you. Do not expect others to see what you see.

   Many people walk by sight and not by faith. However, believers see things differently: "We walk by faith, not by sight" (2 Corinthians 5:7, KJV).

5. **Plant your seeds in fertile ground.** For example, if you wanted to grow oranges, you would not try to grow them in Michigan. The climate there is not the best for growing such things. You would go to a warmer climate like that of Florida, where such growth is prevalent. You have to place yourself in an environment that is conducive to what you desire.

6. **Nurture your dreams with daily prayer, meditation, and study.** Whatever you aspire to do, get to know it so well that you achieve it as a natural outgrowth of your everyday life.

7. **Pursue your dream.** "Faith without works is dead" (James 2:26, KJV).

8. **Endure.** "Be not deceived; God is not mocked: for whatsoever a man soweth, that shall he also reap" (Galatians 6:7, KJV).

Just because things do not seem to be happening for you right now, that does not mean they are not going to happen at all. Continue planting, watering, fertilizing, and exposing your dreams to the L.I.G.H.T. (Life In God's Holy Truth). Your harvest is coming. God's delays are not denials.

Acronym to Remember: **B.E.Y.O.N.D. L.I.M.I.T.A.T.I.O.N.** (**B**oldly **E**mbrace **Y**our **O**wn **N**atural **D**estiny. **L**ife **I**s **M**easured **I**n **T**hought; **A**bundant **T**hinking **I**s **O**f **N**ecessity)

Verse to Remember:
"As he thinks within himself so he is" (Proverbs 23:7, NASB).

Questions of the Day:
• Where do you see yourself in ten years?

• Where do you see yourself in the next five years?

• Where do you see yourself in the next two years?

• Where do you see yourself in the next six months?

DAY 12

G od
I s
A lmighty;
N ow
T ake the
S tuff!

None of those who have faith in God will ever be disgraced for trusting him.

–Psalm 25:3, TLB

The law of nature is, Do the thing, and you shall have the power; but they who do not the thing have not the power.[1]

–Ralph Waldo Emerson

My friend Bob Hill has owned and operated a number of successful radio stations throughout the Southeast. Though a Christian himself, Bob is hesitant to hire other Christians. He says, "I have seen too many of our Christian brothers and sisters hide their weaknesses and fears behind their illusionary Christian armor." Bob has seen many of the Christians that he has hired for sales positions wait for the phone to ring as opposed to going out and seizing opportunity. He says, "They spend more time talking about God than they do demonstrating his power." But he adds, "When I find a believer who is aggressive, I hire him."

Is Bob's method wrong? Not according to the Word of God. "Having a form of godliness, but denying the power thereof: from such turn away" (2 Timothy 3:5, KJV). People may not always live what they pro-

---

1. *Ralph Waldo Emerson. From "Compensation," in* Emerson's Essays, *83. Copyright 1926 by Thomas Y. Crowell Company, Inc. Permission to reprint granted by Harper-Collins Publishers.*

fess, but they will always live what they believe. Many Christians who profess to be Christians don't really believe.

Bob is aggressive. His workday starts before daybreak and doesn't end until nighttime. Bob believes that he can accomplish all things through Christ. His Christian witness is in his success. It allows him to be a blessing to others. It is common for Bob to give of his money to help others in his community who are in a financial bind. People call him almost daily for help. Bob wouldn't have the money to help if he didn't have the courage to go out and earn it.

"The LORD said to Moses, 'Send some men to explore the land of Canaan, which I am giving to the Israelites. From each ancestral tribe send one of its leaders'" (Numbers 13:1, NIV). Moses did as the Lord commanded and sent the men out. When they returned, they told him, "We went into the land to which you sent us, and it does flow with milk and honey! Here is its fruit. But the people who live there are powerful, and the cities are fortified and very large" (Numbers 13:27-28, NIV).

Instead of leaning on God's promise, the Israelites were looking for reasons why they couldn't take what rightfully belonged to them.

> Caleb silenced the people before Moses and said, "We should go up and take possession of the land, for we can certainly do it."
>
> But the men who had gone up with him said, "We can't attack those people; they are stronger than we are." And they spread among the Israelites a bad report about the land they had explored. They said, "The land we explored devours those living in it. All the people we saw there are of great size. . . . We seemed like grasshoppers in our own eyes, and we looked the same to them."
>
> —Numbers 13:30-33, NIV

These weak leaders saw themselves as weak in their own sight. "For as he thinks within himself, so he is" (Proverbs 23:7, NASB).

The people complained. "'Why is the LORD bringing us to this land only to let us fall by the sword? Our wives and children will be taken as plunder. Wouldn't it be better for us to go back to Egypt?' And they said to each other, 'We should choose a leader and go back to Egypt'" (Numbers 14:3-4, NIV).

Their complaining put them in an uncomfortable rut. Their mindsets were so negative that they refused to take what God had given them. "It is because the LORD was not able to bring this people into the land he swore to give them that he has slaughtered them in the wilderness" (Numbers 14:16, NRSV).

God wants to deliver many of us into success and prosperity, but God doesn't do so because we are afraid to boldly say and do what we ought. We want to remain in the captivity of the jobs we hate. We say such things as "I know salespeople can make a lot of money, but I can't get out there and cold-call. I can't handle rejection." We say such things as "I want to own my own business, but it's too hard." So we don't even research to see what it will take to succeed. We just accept less than our privilege and say, "I'm just trusting in the Lord." Trusting in the Lord doesn't mean accepting less than your privilege. It means boldly pursuing a dream that God has placed in your heart.

"Faith without works is dead" (James 2:26, KJV). God is almighty. You can do all things through Christ if you believe. Happiness, success, wealth, and prosperity are all yours for the taking. The size of your dream does not matter. God is bigger than any perceived G.I.A.N.T.S. (God Is Almighty; Now Take the Stuff!).

Acronym to Remember: G.I.A.N.T.S.
(God Is Almighty; Now Take the Stuff!)

Verse to Remember:
"None who have faith in God will ever be disgraced for trusting him" (Psalm 25:3, TLB).

Questions of the Day:
- Read Numbers 13:27-33. Why do you think the men gave a false report?

- Describe a time when you failed to follow through on something because of fear of failure.

- Read 2 Timothy 1:7. If God has not given you a spirit of fear, where do you think your fear came from? And why is it there?

- What does trusting in the Lord mean?

- The next time fear comes into your mind, what will you do, and why?

DAY 13

F orsaking
A ll,
I 'll
T rust
H im

Then Jesus told his disciples, "If any want to become my followers, let them deny themselves and take up their cross and follow me. For those who want to save their life will lose it, and those who lose their life for my sake will find it. For what will it profit them if they gain the whole world but forfeit their life? Or what will they give in return for their life?"

—Matthew 16:24-26, NRSV

During a time in the past when I had multiple streams of income to make my life very comfortable, I relied very little on God. I had it "together"—so I thought. And then I got a wake-up call.

I was out of town on business, and while in a meeting, I received a call on my cell phone that went into my voice mail. It was from the company's Vice-President of Sales. He left a message that said, "Ed, call me as soon as possible. There has been some restructuring in the organization that will affect you personally."

I called him and he inquired, "Ed, how are you?" I answered, "Not well based on the message you left." I asked, "What's going on?" He said, "We are merging two of our company divisions together and eliminating two Regional Sales Manager positions. Both are in your division. Unfortunately, yours is one of them. Fly back to Atlanta as soon as possible so that we can discuss your exit package."

In an instant, my life was changed. At the time it appeared to be for the worst—I had just lost a six-figure job! I was numb. What was I going to tell my wife? I called one of my best friends for consolation. I told him what happened and he responded, "Congratulations!" At the time, his response peeved me to the highest level.

It appeared that my life had taken a bad turn and was beginning to fall apart. Shortly after that I learned that while I had been traveling, my wife had been carrying on an affair. I later learned she was pregnant and that the child was not ours.

During this time period, I also learned that a business partner had been usurping funds that belonged to me. The amount was in the tens of thousands of dollars. I needed the money and they were not able to repay it. I wanted to sue them, but the Holy Spirit told me "No."

I believe that God allowed these things to occur in my life because he was displeased with me. For seven years, I had deviated from the path of my calling to pursue other interests. My calling took a back seat. I got a taste of a little money and began to drift farther and farther from my calling. I almost lost focus. Unknowingly, I was departing from God as well.

"The Lord disciplines those he loves, and he punishes everyone he accepts as a son" (Hebrews 12:6, NIV). Because God loved me so much, he provided a wake-up call. Fortunately, I got the message! However, it came with a price.

Oftentimes, we will strike deals with the world instead of trusting God. He called me to be a minister of the gospel, reaching outside the walls of the church as a speaker and writer. However, I wanted the guarantee of a high salary, so I leaned on corporate America, which was convenient at that time. Foolishly, I did not trust in God. I trusted more in the money on which the words "In God we trust" are inscribed. This behavior offended God. "Thus Saith the Lord; Cursed be the man that trusteth in man, and maketh flesh his arm, and whose heart departeth from the LORD" (Jeremiah 17:5, KJV). Things go awry when you focus more on your business than you do on God's business.

In 2 Chronicles 16 King Asa struck a deal with the king of Syria and trusted him more than he trusted God. He thought that God could not or would not help him so he took matters into his own hands. God is displeased with us when we fail to trust him and rely instead on the "arm of flesh," which is simply our jobs, money, spouses, family name, credentials, status, etc. As a result, we throw ourselves out of the protection of God.

Hanani the prophet came to Asa and told him: "Because you relied on the king of Aram and not on the LORD your God, the army of the king of Aram has escaped from your hand" (2 Chronicles 16:7, NIV).

Our armies of Aram are the things we think will protect us. When the going gets tough everything that is not of God will leave you. Because Asa refused to receive this wisdom, he was diseased in his feet. The feet represent our thinking and understanding. "Though his disease was severe, even in his illness he did not seek help from the LORD, but only from the physicians" (2 Chronicles 16:12, NIV).

Jesus tells us, "You will know the truth, and the truth will make you free" (John 8:32, NASB). As Christians, those of us who read the Bible know the truth, but we don't understand it. I once heard Larry Huch say, "You shall understand the truth and the truth shall set you free." I agree. That's why it is so important to study the Bible, read books to increase understanding, and learn from the experiences of others. "Wisdom is the principal thing; therefore get wisdom; and with all thy getting get understanding" (Proverbs 4:7, KJV).

You cannot walk into the promises of God with diseased feet (thinking). When your thinking is disease-free, God can order your steps and "(e)very place that the sole of your foot shall tread upon, that have I given unto you, as I said unto Moses" (Joshua 1:3, KJV).

When my friend John Jean-Pierre congratulated me on losing my job, I did not understand at the time what he meant. He later explained that he felt I had been wasting my God-given talents and abilities serving myself instead of God. He believed that time away from the distractions of a job outside of my calling would force me to hear from God and do exactly what God intended for me to do. He was right.

I was forced to tune into God more and listen closer to his voice. I was in a desperate situation and needed direction from God to get through my wilderness experience.

We can avoid having to be stripped by simply choosing to trust God from the start, obeying God's commands and directives. I learned this lesson the hard way. I pray that in the course of your reading, you will spare yourself much grief by exercising F.A.I.T.H. (Forsaking All, I'll Trust Him). God knows what he's doing.

Acronym to Remember: **F.A.I.T.H.**
(**F**orsaking **A**ll, **I**'ll **T**rust **H**im)

Verse to Remember:
"If any want to become my followers, let them deny themselves and take up their cross and follow me" (Matthew 16:24, NRSV).

Questions of the Day:
- In what way, if any, are you displeasing God?

- Identify some ways that you have noticed God trying to get your attention.

- Read Jeremiah 17:5. What is the consequence of trusting more in others than in God?

- What are some ways that you have paid the price?

- What will you do differently?

- What did you learn from today's reading and with whom can you share it?

DAY 14

F rame
O f
R eference
C hanges/Creates
E xperiences

I'll put all this behind me,
I'll look on the bright side and force a smile.

—Job 9:27, The Message

In 1987 I had an opportunity to purchase a Salvador Dali limited, signed, and numbered copy of his famous painting entitled *Abraham Lincoln*. The asking price was $900. It was a bargain and I had the money. However, my values were much different back then. I thought $900 for a picture was a waste of money.

Salvador Dali died not long after. That picture is now worth at least ten times the amount I was quoted. I missed not only an investment opportunity but also a chance to purchase something of significant aesthetic value that I later would have appreciated.

The power of that picture still resonates in my soul today. It was a lesson about change. I looked at the picture straight on and clearly saw George Washington. I remember saying, "That's not Abraham Lincoln."

Someone said to me, "Move about fifteen degrees to the left and squint your eyes."

I moved fifteen degrees to the left, squinted my eyes, and clearly saw Abraham Lincoln.

Our Frames Of Reference Change/Create Experiences. The *frame* refers to your state of mind or the way you look at things. *Reference* is defined as "direction of attention." God wants us to direct our attention to faith in God. "Through faith we understand that the worlds were

71

framed by the word of God, so that things which are seen were not made of things which do appear" (Hebrews 11:3, KJV).

The intended message in Dali's *Abraham Lincoln* required faith in order to see it. I had to believe that Lincoln was indeed in the picture. This caused me to look for him. To find him, I had to change my frame of reference. The change in the way I looked at the picture created the experience. I indeed saw Abraham Lincoln.

Likewise, to see God requires faith. "For he who comes to God must believe that He is and that He is a rewarder of those who seek Him" (Hebrews 11:6, NASB).

Many of us are of the frame of mind that we have to physically die and go to heaven to experience God. You might go to heaven if you die. However, if your frame of reference is limited to such a myopic view, you might wait a long time to experience the presence of God.

Back in the days of Solomon, God dwelt in buildings called temples. After Christ came, God moved. God now dwells in us. "You realize, don't you, that you are the temple of God, and God himself is present in you?" (1 Corinthians 3:16, The Message).

If you are looking for God in a building that you call "church," let me tell you, you won't find God there. God has moved. You are church. "God dwells deeply within us" (1 John 4:11, The Message).

To sustain ourselves, we have to learn to listen to the word of God. In 1 Kings 17 we read how God directed Elijah to a brook that supplied Elijah with water. God ordered the ravens to feed him there. Elijah obeyed God, and his needs were met. However, sometime later the brook dried up. Did this mean that God was no longer looking out for him? No. God simply moved his food supply.

Elijah could not depend upon the brook for water; he needed to look to God. Once again, Elijah listened to the word of God, and guess what? God continued to provide every day for his needs. Many people exclude God and look to "brooks" such as jobs, bank accounts, spouses, social status, and the government to supply their needs. Natural circumstances can dry up those brooks in an instant. It's important that you not look to your "brook" to supply your needs but instead look to God. For many of us, this requires a major shift in thinking.

An unwillingness to change frames of reference and look to God has for centuries caused many people to miss God's movement. A great many people during Christ's time missed the Messiah because they were unwilling to do a paradigm shift and recognize that the Messiah had come in the form of a man, born to a virgin named Mary. Jesus' earthly father was a lowly carpenter. The people during Christ's time were expecting the Messiah to come as a king, in accordance with their own limited frame of reference. Had they just changed the way they looked at Jesus, they would have seen his glory, power, and majesty.

Change is inevitable, but growth is optional. In order to grow, you must change. It starts with your thinking.

Believe that God is. Start looking for the divine in your present situations, even the painful ones, and you might find God. After Jesus had been crucified, "when the disciples were together, with the doors locked for fear of the Jews, Jesus came and stood among them and said, 'Peace be with you!' After he said this, he showed them his hands and side. The disciples were overjoyed when they saw the Lord" (John 20:19-20, NIV).

The disciples received 20/20 spiritual vision. They were able to recognize Jesus by his wounds. When he was crucified, he was pierced through his hands and his side. It was the force of God that allowed him to endure. Although it was painful, he focused on his purpose. It was also the force of God that resurrected him. What would have happened if he looked at being beaten, spat on, and crucified as just too much to bear and so refused to go through with it?

You might be waiting on God to pour out a blessing on you, but God is waiting on you to shift your focus so you can realize that you're already blessed. You must move in order to experience the blessings that God has for you. "Seek, and ye shall find" (Matthew 7:7, KJV).

God is in your history. Christ is in your life. The Holy Spirit is operative in your affairs. The F.O.R.C.E. is with you!

Acronym to Remember: **F.O.R.C.E.**
(**Frame Of Reference Changes/Creates Experiences**)

Verse to Remember:
"I'll put all this behind me, I'll look on the bright side and force a smile" (Job 9:27, The Message).

Questions of the Day:
- What opportunities can you recall missing because of a limited frame of reference?

- What does God want our primary frame of reference to be?

- Do you see God in Christ?

- Do you see Christ in yourself?

- When others look at you, do they see Christ?

- What painful personal experiences, if any, do you recall being able to see Christ in?

- What did you gain from this lesson, and with whom can you share it?

God, male/female relationships, and love

DAY 15

S in
I s
C arnal
K nowledge

I will make you sick, striking you down,
Desolating you because of your sins.

—Micah 6:13, NASB

Have you ever looked back over your life and asked, "Why do I seem to make so many wrong decisions? How did I arrive at such a pathetic state in my life?" Instead of choosing what God has for us, we sometimes lean on our own understanding and choose incorrectly. When guided by carnal thinking, we are led to make costly mistakes.

King David had a close relationship with God. God was with him and was his inspiration. He accomplished incredible feats, won numerous battles, and wrote many powerful psalms. His most famous is the twenty-third psalm. "The LORD is my shepherd; I shall not want" (Psalm 23:1, KJV). Spiritually, he had an awareness that everything he needed God had already provided, until "one evening David got up from his bed and walked around on the roof of the palace. From the roof he saw a woman bathing. The woman was very beautiful" (2 Samuel 11:2, NIV).

She was beautiful, the epitome of divine craftsmanship. Allowing himself to be led by the flesh instead of the Spirit, David perhaps took his inspired psalm out of context and said something like, "The Lord is my shepherd; I see what I want."

"So David sent and inquired about the woman. And one said, 'Is this not Bathsheba, the daughter of Eliam, the wife of Uriah the Hittite?' " (2 Samuel 11:3, NASB). The fact that she was married to one of his most loyal servants did not stop David from pursuing her. Why? He allowed himself to completely surrender to his flesh. In a continued state of erroneous thinking, he seems to have rewritten Psalm 23:2 to say, "I maketh me to lie down with someone else's wife; I leadeth me into unrighteousness." The devil didn't make him do it.

"Then David sent messengers to get her. She came to him, and he slept with her.... Then she went back home. The woman conceived and sent word to David, saying, 'I am pregnant' " (2 Samuel 11:4-5, NIV).

Falling deeper into sin, David inquired of his carnal mind, "What should I do now?" To cover up his transgression, David sent for Bathsheba's husband, Uriah, from the battlefield. He thought that Uriah, upon returning from the battlefield, would go and sleep with his wife, so that everyone would think that Bathsheba's husband was the father.

Uriah was such a loyal servant that he slept at the entrance of the palace instead. So David chose to get rid of Uriah. He ordered Joab, Uriah's commander, "Put Uriah in the front line where the fighting is fiercest. Then withdraw from him so he will be struck down and die" (2 Samuel 11:15, NIV). David had Uriah murdered to cover up his own sin.

What David had done displeased God. The LORD sent the prophet Nathan to David to rebuke him. "This is what the LORD says: 'Out of your own household I am going to bring calamity upon you. Before your very eyes I will take your wives and give them to one who is close to you, and he will lie with your wives in broad daylight. You did it in secret, but I will do this thing in broad daylight" (2 Samuel 12:11-12, NIV).

God spared David's life because he repented, but there still were consequences. The Lord struck the child that Uriah's wife had borne to David, and he became ill and died (2 Samuel 12:15-18). Later, David's son Amnon fell in love with his own sister. Unable to control his lust, he raped his sister. Absalom, another of David's sons, murdered his own brother to avenge his sister's honor. Absalom later tried to kill David and take his kingdom. He also openly slept with David's wives (2 Samuel 16:21-22).

God forgave David, but his household was dysfunctional. Often the dysfunction we find in our families today is the result of the sins of our parents. The dysfunction is passed from generation to generation.

A life of sin is like walking down a spiral staircase. You don't realize you have reached the bottom until your feet actually touch the ground.

Running around feels like fun, until you realize there is hell to pay. "Work hard for sin … and your pension is death" (Romans 6:23, The Message).

We all have weaknesses in our lives that could cause us to walk down the spiral staircase of life, trip and spin out of control, and fall hard and break up our families. To this end we should pray, "Do not let us enter into temptation, but deliver us from evil" (Matthew 6:13, Ancient Eastern Text).

David and his sons had weaknesses for beautiful women. Many men have this same weakness. Some struggle with it, while others give in to it and severely harm themselves and their families for many generations. In today's society, women are just as prone as men to sexual impropriety.

Some of us have other areas of weakness. "Guard your heart, for it affects everything you do" (Proverbs 4:23, NLT). God wants you to do some soul-searching and identify problem areas in your life where you may be entertaining the thought of sin. The weaknesses you identify must be addressed before they cause you to commit spiritual suicide on an installment plan. Your whole family, for many generations, could suffer the consequences of your wrong action.

As I mentioned earlier, my wife had an affair. She and her paramour conceived a child. We separated and are now divorced. It was the most painful event of my life. I asked God, "Why did you allow infidelity to touch my household?" God showed me why. The truth is that infidelity was already upon my household. I was born as a result of my father having an affair with my mother. My late stepmother, Mattie Gray, forgave my father, and her love for God made her civil toward my mother. She never once negatively brought up to me the circumstances surrounding my birth.

Not until my adulthood did my stepmother and I even discuss my father's infidelity, the painful emotions my stepmother felt when she learned that my father had conceived a child with another woman during their relationship, and the drama that followed. In a conversation I had with my stepmother on my twenty-eighth birthday, we discussed those things and the shame that we both carried.

My stepmother was ashamed that at the time I was conceived and for many years prior, she and my dad were, as she put it, "shacking," which means living together in sin. Not long after I was born, they legalized their marriage.

Although I was raised primarily by my mother, I had a closer relationship with my stepmother. From my infancy, I lived with my mother and my older brother and sister. I visited my dad and stepmother every weekend. The facts that my stepmother had no other children and that both she and my father were in their late fifties when I was born might have contributed to her acceptance of me.

What my parents did was wrong. Someone had to pay the price—my father's seed, me. I carried the cross in the shame I felt growing up. I paid by experiencing the same kind of pain my stepmother felt. It's a pain that I wish upon no one, especially my future children and grandchildren.

Had I known earlier that this was the cross I would have to bear, I would have fallen on my face and prayed to the Father as Jesus did, "O my Father, if it be possible, let this cup pass from me" (Matthew 26:39, KJV).

"My people are destroyed for lack of knowledge" (Hosea 4:6, KJV). We destroy our reputations and families because we don't realize that the law of reciprocity is as real as the law of gravity.

Infidelity is not only selfishness. It is also a sin against God. "Don't be misled: No one makes a fool of God. What a person plants, he will harvest. The person who plants selfishness, ignoring the needs of others—ignoring God!—harvests a crop of weeds" (Galatians 6:7-8, The Message). Those weeds will grow wild throughout your family.

If the spirit of lust is upon your family, you have the power to break the curse. It starts by recognizing signs of lust in your heart and then turning away from them. The spirit of lust shows up in many ways: perhaps a "wandering eye" or an attraction to pornography. If you see signs of lust within you, pray and ask God to remove those desires from your heart. Ask God to cleanse you from all unrighteousness (see Psalm 51). You don't have to remain S.I.C.K. unless you choose to. "Choose life in order that you may live, you and your descendants" (Deuteronomy 30:19, NASB).

Pray and ask God to remove the curse.

Acronym to Remember: **S.I.C.K.**
(**S**in **I**s **C**arnal **K**nowledge)

Wild Weeds in The Family

81

Verse to Remember:
"If my people, which are called by my name, shall humble themselves, and pray, and seek my face, and turn from their wicked ways; then I will hear from heaven, and will forgive their sin, and will heal their land" (2 Chronicles 7:14, KJV).

Questions of the Day:
• What are some areas of your life that seem prone to sin?

• In David's family, immorality was rampant. What patterns of sin have you noticed in your family?

• How long has such behavior been in your family?

• Has anyone recognized it as a problem?

- How have you personally been affected by it?

- What did you learn from today's reading, and with whom can you share it?

DAY 16

A n
I ntimate
R elationship

So God created humankind in his image, in the image of God he created them; male and female he created them.

—Genesis 2:7, NRSV

The word "spirit" is translated from the Hebrew word *neshamah,* whose root word means "divine inspiration, intellect, soul, spirit."[1] When God breathed into Adam, the original man, he was immediately in relationship with God; they shared the same spirit. Adam came alive. He was inspired. To *inspire* means "to breathe into." God breathed into Adam, so Adam was divinely inspired.

Divine inspiration comes with blessings. When God breathed into Adam, he became a somebody; he was given significance. "God blessed them [the first humans], and God said unto them, Be fruitful, and multiply, and replenish the earth, and subdue it" (Genesis 1:28, KJV). Adam and Eve were given dominion over the earth and everything in it.

Adam lived and breathed God. In other words, Adam's lifestyle was prosperous. The word *prosperous,* in its Hebrew root *yashar,* means "right, pleasant, or esteemed." Whatever Adam needed and wanted was his for the taking, because he was in right standing with God.

God blessed him with a mate. "The LORD God said, 'It is not good for the man to be alone. I will make a helper suitable for him'" (Genesis 2:18, NIV). God made a woman, and she became his wife (Genesis 2:22-25). God blessed them and provided for them. It was an intimate relationship—A.I.R.

---

1. *James Strong,* The Exhaustive Concordance of the Bible *(Nashville: Abindgon, 1890),* "Greek Dictionary of the New Testament," *#5397.*

Adam's intimacy with God was lost when he and his wife chose to disobey God. Eve listened to a voice other than God's. She was lured by the charm of the crafty serpent.

> He said to the woman, "Did God really say, 'You must not eat from any tree in the garden'?"
>
> The woman said to the serpent, "We may eat fruit from the trees in the garden, but God did say, 'You must not eat fruit from the tree that is in the middle of the garden, and you must not touch it, or you will die.'"

—Genesis 3:1-2, NIV

The crafty serpent still comes to us in the form of temptation. I watched a crafty serpent attempt to prey on a married woman. He asked, "Are you married?"

She said, "Yes I am."

He then proceeded with, "Are you happily married?" as if her marital unhappiness was justification for breaking covenant with God.

The serpent told Eve a lie to rationalize why it was okay to disobey God's commandment. "'You will not surely die,' the serpent said to the woman. 'For God knows that when you eat of it your eyes will be opened, and you will be like God, knowing good and evil'" (Genesis 3:4, NIV).

The fruit looked good, and the woman ate of it. "She also gave some to her husband, who was with her, and he ate it" (Genesis 3:6, NIV). The trust was broken and the bond that held the relationship between them and their God was shattered. Their lives were changed in an instant. Now they knew shame, which had been nonexistent in their lives before they sinned (Genesis 3:7).

Pain and suffering came into their lives. The pain of childbirth increased because of the original sin (Genesis 3:16). The things that the man wanted now came with a price.

> The very ground is cursed because of you;
>   getting food from the ground
> Will be as painful as having babies is for your wife;
>   you'll be working in pain all your life long.
> The ground will sprout thorns and weeds,
>   you'll get your food working the hard way,

Planting and tilling and harvesting,
    sweating in the fields from dawn to dusk,
Until you return to that ground yourself, dead and buried;
    you started out as dirt, you'll end up dirt.
                 —Genesis 3:17-19, The Message

Life in the A.I.R. (An Intimate Relationship) with God was pleasant. Adam and Eve's address in the Garden of Eden was 111 Easy Street. They had it made until they sinned and were cast out. A spiritual death occurred; they were separated from God's presence. Eternal, physical, and spiritual life for us was in God's original plan. However, sin caused us to die before our time.

"Sin entered the world through one man, and death through sin, and in this way death came to all men, because all sinned" (Romans 5:12, NIV). Just as we inherited physical life from our ancestors Adam and Eve, so we also inherited spiritual death.

Entertainment mogul Kenny ("Baby Face") Edmonds wrote a song entitled "Breathe Again," which Toni Braxton sang and popularized. The song is about a dependent relationship. Braxton said, "I promise you that if love ends I shall never breathe again."

God's love for us will never end. However, if we lose knowledge of God and knowledge of God's love, we lose A.I.R. (An Intimate Relationship) with God.

Adam and Eve's knowledge of God was lost. They were L.O.S.T. (Leaning On Stupid/Sinful Things). They tried to hide from God (Genesis 3:7-8). We still do the same thing. Like a toddler who covers her face, believing that because she can't see you, you can't see her, we think that because we can't see God when we sin, God doesn't see us. We inherited this stupid/sinful notion.

Fortunately, through Christ, we can reclaim our knowledge of God. We can regain our intimate relationship with him, living and breathing God in our lives. This occurs by conforming our minds so that they reflect the mind of Christ, as discussed throughout this book.

This requires discipline. If you truly want to breathe again, you must love God and depend upon God as if God is the air you breathe. "'Love the Lord your God with all your heart and with all your soul and with all your mind.' This is the first and greatest commandment" (Matthew 22:37, NIV).

Many of us say we love God, but we break God's commandments. We lie, cheat, steal, bear false witness, and assassinate the character of others by gossiping. Adultery, which is forbidden in the commandments, occurs in many marriages, and fornication, which is also forbidden, is a societal norm. These sins occur even among us church folks who claim to love the Lord. We have been lying to ourselves. We don't love the Lord; we're not even in relationship with the Lord.

Because we are out of relationship with God, our relationships with each other also suffer. We do wrong to each other when we are not in true relationship with God, because we have nothing that we believe is worthwhile to hang onto to keep us from going astray.

Referring to the second most important commandment, Jesus said, "'Love your neighbor as yourself.' All the Law and the Prophets hang on these two commandments" (Matthew 22:39-40, NIV).

If you want to breathe the life of God, you can no longer do what you want to do, if what you want to do goes against God's Word or hurts someone else. Sure, everybody does it, but the way of the world is death. The way of God is life. Jesus said, "I came that they may have life, and have it abundantly" (John 10:10, NASB). Choose life by conforming your mind to the mind of Christ. "Be not conformed to this world: but be ye transformed by the renewing of your mind" (Romans 12:2, KJV).

I am learning that when you begin to conform to God's mind, you will begin to flow in the things of God. The word *affluence* means "to flow." Divine inspiration will flow through you. This book is a byproduct of the divine flow that is available to all who are willing to change.

If your life is difficult and you feel that you can't breathe emotionally, financially, or spiritually, ask God for A.I.R. (An Intimate Relationship). Before continuing with your reading, stop now and take some moments to pray the following prayer:

Eternal God, you said that you would never leave or forsake me. I know that you are with me now. Lord, I ask that you forgive me for leaving and forsaking you. My life has been difficult without you. *(Tell God what has been going on in your life—cry out to God!)*

a prayer

87

Because of my sin, I have felt shame and guilt, just as my ancestors Adam and Eve felt in your presence. Because of my shame, I have not felt the liberty that you said I would have in Christ, because I have not been living under his grace. I have been afraid to disclose my inner self even to those closest to me. I have lived in a fear that is not of you. I ask you now to release me from the bondage of sin, and I will walk in your integrity.

Yes, I have sinned, and I acknowledge my sin before you and ask your forgiveness. I accept your forgiveness, and I forgive myself. I ask Jesus to come into my life as never before. I inhale the breath of life. *(Pause and breathe in God.)* I will live and breathe you all the days of my life.

In Jesus' name. Amen.

Through Jesus we are provided A.I.R. (Adam Is Resurrected). If you have accepted Jesus into your life, you are now alive spiritually because you breathe clean

A.I.R.—An Intimate Relationship with God through Christ.

Acronym to Remember: A.I.R.
(An Intimate Relationship)

Verse to Remember:
"So God created humankind in his image, in the image of God he created them; male and female he created them" (Genesis 2:7, NRSV).

Questions of the Day:
• How was the original couple's intimacy with God lost?

- How did their lifestyle change after sin?

- What happened to Adam and Eve's spirit after they sinned?

- Read Romans 5:12. How were you affected?

- How can we regain our intimacy with God?

- What did you learn from today's reading, and with whom can you share it?

DAY 17

G od
O rdained;
N othing
E lse

I cry out, "My splendor is gone! Everything I had hoped for from the LORD is lost!"

–Lamentations 3:18, NLT

Webster has five laconic definitions for the word *gone*. They are "ruined; lost; dead; faint; and weak." Whenever we pursue a relationship, career, or any other endeavor that was not God-ordained, we are subject to experiencing ruin or any one of the other disasters mentioned in the four words used to define *gone*. Without God, the final outcome is never good.

My friend Lee had been married and divorced twice. He was engaged to marry a third time. He and his fiancée had gone through twelve weeks of intense premarital counseling. They were attracted to each other and in love (or so they thought). Their pastor called them into his office following a midweek service. The pastor said to Lee, "If you can tell me that she is the one God ordained for you to marry before the foundations of the earth, I will perform the ceremony."

Lee could not honestly say that she was the one God had ordained to be his wife. Nor could his fiancée say the same about him. The pastor said, "If God hasn't said yes, then I can't say yes." He refused to perform the ceremony.

Lee had met the woman God had ordained for him years earlier. However, he paid her no attention. God led him in her direction one day and told him to turn to the right. He turned and saw the woman. God spoke to him and said, "She's your mate."

He asked, "God, could you change your mind?" The Lord brought to his memory Malachi 3:6: "I am the LORD, I change not" (KJV).

Lee had grown accustomed to being led by God in other areas of his life. However, when it came to relationships, he trusted his eyes. He decided to listen to God.

God had also been working in the life of the woman who would become Lee's wife. They both listened to God. The pastor agreed to perform that ceremony, and they are now happily married.

Flesh is flesh, and spirit is spirit. When you make a decision based upon the flesh, it takes things of the flesh to sustain it. If it's money and position that you seek in a mate, there is a possibility you will stray when the money and status are gone or when someone with more of the fleshly things that attract you comes along.

As men, we are usually attracted by physical appearance. Some of us make our decisions based upon looks. When another woman—who is perhaps younger and has a prettier face or more curvaceous body—comes along, we can be tempted.

Love without a spiritual anchor is easily moved. That's why we are told, "Walk not after the flesh, but after the Spirit" (Romans 8:4, KJV).

"For as many as are led by the Spirit of God, they are the sons of God" (Romans 8:14, KJV). Children receive a divine inheritance. In other words, at a set time they receive what God ordained for them to have. Because it is a gift from God, no one can take it. Not so with the flesh. Flesh can get bored. When it does, it looks for new flesh.

Walking in the flesh develops in our youth. Teenagers are notorious for wanting to do what other teenagers are doing. It's called "peer pressure." If other teens are having sex, they are moved to make the same mistake. They will even model other kids' methods of hiding their activities from their parents.

A fourteen-year-old asked her mom to take her and her friends to the mall, drop them off, and pick them up later. She told her mom that they wanted to do some shopping and catch a movie, so she wanted to be picked up five hours later.

Being a good and highly intuitive parent, the mother didn't feel comfortable letting her daughter go, so she told her no.

The teen told her mom, "You don't let me have any freedom. You don't trust me. All the other kids' parents let them go to the mall."

Against her better judgment, the mom let her guard down. She later found out that the girls would make plans to go to the mall to meet boys who were older and had access to cars. They were leaving the mall and going elsewhere to have sex. The family was devastated when they learned that their baby's virginity had been lost.

I deeply regret that I lost my virginity in my sophomore year in high school, which might be late compared to some teens today, many of whom are sexually active before they even get to high school. Sex for me became like an addiction. It created more problems. I skipped school to have sex and my grades dropped.

I had to lie to my parents. My girlfriend lied to her parents. When report cards came out, we had to explain our absences. The truth eventually came out, and it was not pleasant. I did not learn to be led by the Spirit until much later in life. Had I known then what I know now, many of the relationship problems I had as an adult could have been avoided. The Spirit, instead of the flesh, would have guided me.

The "everybody else" cry is the spiritual anesthesia the devil uses to numb our spiritual senses. You are a child of God. You have been set aside for a divine purpose. The devil does not want you to fulfill your mission. He can only get you to mess up if you consent. Being led by the flesh instead of the Spirit is a choice that causes you to err. Until you allow yourself to be guided by the Spirit, you will continue to make mistakes. It could even cost you your life. God will restore you if you repent, ask for forgiveness, disassociate yourself from the wrong influences, and stop doing what you were doing.

The "everybody else" attack is nothing new. The children of Israel used it thousands of years ago to refute living God's way and to choose living according to the warped values of everybody else.

> The elders of Israel gathered together and came to Samuel at Ramah. They said to him, "You are old, and your sons do not walk in your ways; now appoint a king to lead us, such as all other nations have."...
>
> This displeased Samuel; so he prayed to the LORD. And the LORD told him: "Listen to all that the people are saying to you; it is not you they have rejected, but they have rejected me as their king."
>
> —1 Samuel 8:4-7, NIV

Through Samuel, God warned them of how they would be used and abused by the king who would reign over them (1 Samuel 8:9-18). "But the people refused to listen to Samuel. 'No!' they said. 'We want a king over us. Then we will be like all the other nations, with a king to lead us and to go out before us and fight our battles'" (1 Samuel 8:19-20, NIV).

"The LORD answered, 'Listen to them and give them a king'" (1 Samuel 8:22, NIV). The children of Israel lived to regret it.

Just as the children of Israel became slaves to the Egyptians, so many of us have become slaves to sin. Choose to accept less than your privilege, and God will let you have it.

"Eye hath not seen, nor ear heard, neither have entered into the heart of man, the things which God hath prepared for them that love him. But God hath revealed them unto us by the Spirit: for the Spirit searcheth all things, yea, the deep things of God" (1 Corinthians 2:9-10, KJV). Choose to be led by the Spirit, and the flesh is G.O.N.E. (God Ordained, Nothing Else), and you will never accept less than your privilege.

Acronym to Remember: **G.O.N.E.**
(**G**od **O**rdained; **N**othing **E**lse)

Verse to Remember:
"Walk not after the flesh, but after the Spirit" (Romans 8:4, KJV).

Questions of the Day:
• What does it take to sustain the flesh?

- Read Romans 8:4. Why do you think we are told to walk after the Spirit and not after the flesh?

- What mistakes have you made as a result of walking after the flesh, and what did it cost you?

- What successes have you had as a result of walking after the Spirit?

DAY 18

A

L ife lived

I n

G od's

N ame

E scapes

D eath

Whatsoever ye shall ask in my name, that will I do, that the Father may be glorified in the Son.

—John 14:13, KJV

Webster defines the word *align* as "to bring into agreement or close cooperation." A.L.I.G.N. (A Life lived In God's Name) is the result of reading God's Word, agreeing with it, and abiding in it. "If you abide in Me, and My words abide in you, ask whatever you wish, and it shall be done for you" (John 15:7, NASB).

When you align with God, God provides everything you could ever wish for. God even tells you what to pray for. "We do not know what we ought to pray for, but the Spirit himself intercedes for us with groans that words cannot express. And he who searches our hearts knows the mind of the Spirit, because the Spirit intercedes for the saints in accordance with God's will" (Romans 8:26-27, NIV).

During the writing of this book, I was inspired in my Bible reading by the following passage: "And when they had prayed, the place where they had gathered together was shaken, and they were filled with the Holy Spirit and began to speak the word of God with boldness" (Acts 4:31, NASB).

One morning in prayer, I asked God to fill me with the Holy Spirit. He answered my prayer, and I began to speak in tongues. He can do the same thing for you if you ask. "If you then, being evil, know how to give good gifts to your children, how much more will your heavenly Father give the Holy Spirit to those who ask Him?" (Luke 11:13, NASB).

I began to pray regularly in the Spirit for ten to thirty minutes a day. My spirit must have been praying for increased creativity and clarity of insight. The volume of creativity has been increased. The Holy Spirit wakes me up regularly in the early morning just to catch the outpouring, which flows like a river.

Right now it is 2:33 A.M., and this is the second time since going to bed last night that God has awakened me to tell me what to write. Such occurrences now happen frequently in my life. I have seen an incredible outpouring of creative wealth. This kind of outpouring is also available to you in your calling if you align your thoughts, words, and actions with God's and flow with them.

"At Gibeon the LORD appeared to Solomon during the night in a dream, and God said, 'Ask for whatever you want me to give you'" (1 Kings 3:5, NIV). Solomon asked for wisdom so that he might better perform the job he was assigned as king.

> The Lord was pleased that Solomon had asked for this. So God said to him, "Since you have asked for this and not for long life or wealth for yourself, nor have you asked for the death of your enemies but for discernment in administering justice, I will do what you have asked. I will give you a wise and discerning heart, so that there will never have been anyone like you, nor will there ever be."
>
> —1 Kings 3:10-12, NIV

At that time in his life, Solomon was in close cooperation with God. Like most of us, Solomon was not perfect, but he aligned himself with God's Word, "walking in the statutes of David his father: only he sacrificed and burnt incense in high places" (1 Kings 3:3, KJV). God knows that we are not perfect. However, those of us who strive for perfection earn favor with God, even though we sometimes make mistakes.

The Spirit told Solomon what to pray for. The Spirit also searched his heart and saw what other wishes were there. God said, "Moreover, I will give you what you have not asked for—both riches and honor—so that in your lifetime you will have no equal among kings" (1 Kings 3:13, NIV). In verse 14, God even added a stipulation to the agreement that would provide long life: "And if you walk in my ways and obey my statutes and commands as David your father did, I will give you a long life" (NIV).

Jesus said, "The thief comes only to steal and kill and destroy; I have come that they may have life, and have it to the full" (John 10:10, NIV). A.L.I.G.N.E.D. (A Life lived In God's Name Escapes Death). For your obedience, He will bless you in more ways than one.

Acronym to Remember: **A.L.I.G.N.E.D.**
(**A L**ife lived **I**n **G**od's **N**ame **E**scapes **D**eath)

Verse to Remember:
"If you abide in Me, and My words abide in you, ask whatever you wish, and it will be done for you" (John 15:7, NASB).

Questions of the Day:
• Why do you think God appeared to Solomon at Gibeon?

• How closely aligned is your life to God's Word?

• What can you expect as a result of aligning your life to God's will?

• What did you learn from this lesson, and with whom can you share it?

DAY 19

H e
U plifts/Understands,
S upports,
B elieves,
A nd
N ever
D estroys
&
W oman of
I ntegrity,
F aith, &
E xcellence

Find a good spouse, you find a good life—
and even more: the favor of God!

—Proverbs 18:22, The Message

How do you find a wife? I posed this question to God for myself, and God responded, "Be a H.U.S.B.A.N.D. (He Uplifts/Understands, Supports, And Never Destroys)." In other words, a husband encourages and brings out the best in his mate and is careful not to destroy his wife's confidence through disparaging words or infidelity. God told me, "Become the man I intend for you to be, and I will show you your wife."

The same advice applies to women: How do you find a husband? Become the woman God intends for you to be.

Recently I met a woman with whom I am building a relationship that might one day lead to marriage. We have become friends. Because I want to be confident that my motives are pure, I asked God to show me a sign if she is the woman God has intended for me. I prayed, "Let her prove herself as a friend who is honest and of noble character. Also, let her see and understand the value of my ministry."

Sometimes those of us who have difficulty comprehending what God is showing us in the spiritual realm require a sign in the physical realm in order to see that it is from God.

In the book of Genesis, Abraham sent his servant out to look for a wife for his son Isaac. The chief assistant prayed,

> O GOD, God of my master Abraham, make things go smoothly this day; treat my master Abraham well! As I stand here by the spring while the young women of town come out to get water, let the girl to whom I say, "Lower your jug and give me a drink," and who answers, "Drink, and let me also water your camels"—let her be the woman you have picked out for your servant Isaac. Then I'll know that you're working graciously behind the scenes for my master.
>
> —Genesis 24:12-14, The Message

The words were barely out of the servant's mouth before there appeared the woman whom God had chosen for Isaac. She was beautiful, a virgin, and she responded just as the servant had prayed.

The servant met the girl's family and explained his purpose for the visit, to find a wife for his master. He explained all that happened, his prayer and God's response confirming that Rebekah was the one. They all agreed it was from God. With Rebekah's consent, her family allowed her to return with Abraham's servant to meet her husband.

> Rebekah and her young maids mounted the camels and followed the man. The servant took Rebekah and set off for home.
>
> Isaac was living in the Negev. He had just come back from a visit to Beer-lahai-roi. In the evening he went out into the field; while meditating he looked up and saw camels coming. When Rebekah looked up and saw Isaac, she got down from her camel and asked the servant, "Who is that man out in the field coming toward us?"
>
> "That is my master."
>
> She took her veil and covered herself.
>
> —Genesis 24:61-65, The Message

As God was delivering his wife to him, Isaac didn't see her physical beauty, because a veil covered it.

I am growing more confident that I have met the woman God has ordained for me to marry. But it is not her physical appearance that first attracted me. It's not that she isn't attractive. In fact, she is extremely beautiful. But God placed a spiritual veil over her so that I would first see her substance. She is a praying woman with a loving spirit. As I began to observe her in the physical realm, what I had seen first in the spiritual realm was confirmed.

If you want to find the person God has ordained for you, rely exclusively on the inside-out approach. Let God show you in the spiritual realm who God has for you. As you increase your prayer and meditation life and submit to God's ways, God will show you many things that lead to happiness and success. He will show a woman of God the man who is to be her H.U.S.B.A.N.D. (He Uplifts/Understands, Supports, And Never Destroys), and he will show a man of God the woman who is to be his W.I.F.E. (Woman of Integrity, Faith, and Excellence).

Acronym to Remember: **H.U.S.B.A.N.D. & W.I.F.E.** (**He** **U**nderstands, **S**upports, **B**elieves, **A**nd **N**ever **D**estroys; **W**oman of **I**ntegrity, **F**aith, & **E**xcellence)

Verse to Remember:
"Find a good spouse, you find a good life—and even more: the favor of GOD!" (Proverbs 18:22, The Message).

Questions of the Day:
• On what basis did the servant choose Rebekah for Isaac?

- What was Isaac doing when he saw his wife coming?

- What did Rebekah do after the servant revealed who Isaac was?

- What does the above answer suggest to you?

- What did you learn from today's reading, and with whom can you share it?

DAY 20

W oman/Man
O f
V irtue,
E levated
N amesake

He who finds a wife finds what is good
   and receives favor from the LORD.

–Proverbs 18:22, NIV

Have you ever found yourself in what you thought was love? By all indications, the object of your desire was quite a catch. Aesthetically, he or she was pleasing. Intellectually, this person's conversation was stimulating. They wooed you and wounded you. How deep was the C.U.T. (Calamity Unveiling the Truth) when you found out that all that glitters isn't G.O.L.D.—God-ordained love and devotion?

The fabric of a relationship that God has not ordained begins to unravel long before couples get to the altar. The snags are flashes of dishonesty, closed communications, differing values, conflicting philosophies, and sometimes even infidelity—all of which equal built-in tension. Many of us close our eyes to the truth and continue dating a lover who is untrue.

It's like getting in your car and carelessly driving down a busy street, ignoring all the stop signals. It's a reckless journey that, if prolonged, could well lead to a multi-car pileup. You could injure yourself as well as those you love.

Innocent children often get caught in the crossfire of divorce and separation. Family and friends are forced to choose sides. In some cases tragedy occurs. During this writing, I read in the newspaper about a physician in Georgia who murdered his wife. Now their two children are without a mother or a father to raise them.

Somewhere along the way, someone didn't heed the voice of God. Usually, it is before the marriage, sometimes during the marriage. Either way, communication with God was broken.

During the court appearance, the doctor I mentioned earlier brought his Bible to court. The damage of not turning to the Word sooner had already been done. A life was gone. His medical career was over, his children were without their mother, and their father was on his way to prison for life.

What happened? The doctor would not go into detail. He said he wanted to save his children the pain and embarrassment, so he just pleaded guilty.

Thinking carnally instead of spiritually, I have made the wrong selections in relationships by choosing what I wanted instead of asking God whom God had chosen for me. My decision-making was wrong. I looked to the flesh first, which indicated that I, too, was wrong. As I mentioned previously, I considered it a value-added benefit if the woman of my desire also claimed to love God. The fact that I did not allow God to lead me revealed a lack of love toward God on my part.

"Keep thy heart with all diligence; for out of it are the issues of life" (Proverbs 4:23, KJV). As I search my soul, I am able to see that my initial view of the women I dated was ungodly.

Many women with whom I maintained a close friendship had all of the virtues of a wife. They were faithful to God. But they were not providing what a shallow man wanted: sex and a trophy on his arm. Because of this, I was just friends with them, and I dated other women. My lack of complete faithfulness to God at that time made me unworthy of a virtuous woman. We would have been unequally yoked. When you are faithful to God, to accept someone who is not faithful to the Lord is to accept less than your privilege.

One of my best friends, Faith, warned me, "Unless you do things God's way, you are going to get hurt, Ed." She was right. One of the mistakes many of us make is that we want to shift into the benefits of marriage without going through all the gears in God's timing.

There are five gears that can lead to marriage if you are the right person and you find the right person. They are as follows:

- First gear—fellowship
- Second gear—friendship
- Third gear—companionship
- Fourth gear—relationship
- Fifth gear—kinship

Working through the gears is like driving with a stick shift. Each movement is a choice. However, the Holy Spirit shows you when to shift.

During this writing, I drove a Saab convertible with a five-speed manual transmission. The car had a shift arrow that lit up when the engine speed rose to around three thousand RPMs, which is the optimum time to shift. Adherence to the dictates of the shift light helps assure engine safety and the best possible gas mileage.

When you find someone with whom you share a mutual interest, such as joy in reading books, studying the Word of God, or writing, the Holy Spirit may provide you with a sign to shift into fellowship. In this mode, don't seek anything else but fellowship. Share your true feelings with each other, encourage one another, admit your weaknesses, discuss your past, and get to know each other.

We sometimes mess things up when our motives for talking go beyond fellowship. For example, a man sees a woman in a bookstore and he is physically attracted to her. He goes over to her and discusses the book she is reading. Like Satan, the deceiver, he pretends to be interested in the same subject. He's not being led by the Holy Spirit; he's being led by the flesh.

His subsequent actions will have fleshly intentions, which lead to something he hopes for that might not include fellowship. It might begin with getting her phone number. If she isn't Spirit-filled and Spirit-led, she won't recognize his game. Maybe she does, but she might also choose to operate from the flesh instead of the Spirit. Either way, the outcome is the same: life outside the spirit breaks covenant with God.

When you are Spirit-led, God will lead you into shifting into first gear when the person and timing are right. Until God shows you the "green light," remain in neutral. Don't let that person into your heart through fellowship or any of the higher gears. Proverbs 4:23 warns to guard our hearts because our hearts are the source of the issues and wellsprings in our lives.

Fellowship is much deeper than superficial chitchat. It requires openness, sharing who you are, where you are, where you're going, and how you plan to get there. It provides the freedom to share your feelings without being judged. It is in fellowship that you discover a true friend. When the timing is right you can shift to second gear: friendship.

The friendship between a man and the woman God has chosen to be together is like two bodies and one soul even though there is no physical contact. There is a complete openness and trust that includes God. The two of you "look out for one another's interests, not just for your own" (Philippians 2:4, TEV). The Greek word *skopos* surmounts the true meaning of "looking out for one another"; it means "to pay close attention." This is done by taking the time to understand each other's feelings and by being considerate of those feelings. A person who respects your feelings is someone you want to be around. Therefore, friendship prepares you for shifting into third gear: companionship.

Companionship is like a matching pair of shoes. Although one shoe is a left shoe and the other is a right shoe, they complement each other. In this gear the two of you walk together. You accompany each other to places that interest both of you, such as concerts, museums, parks, and movies. In accordance with God's plan, physical intimacy should not occur, because it may cloud the spiritual intimacy. At this level, God may begin leading you into fourth gear: relationship. When God leads you to begin making plans for an engagement, start making plans to shift into fifth gear: kinship.

Dating is indeed like driving a stick-shift car. If you shift too soon or too late, you can cause damage to the car. For best results, look to God and let God show you signs that it is time to shift. Sex is reserved exclusively for fifth gear: kinship. If you shift too soon, your union will be strained from the start, because you are not looking to God for insight but rather to your flesh, which is prone to error.

You have a stronger chance of succeeding in marriage when you go through all the gears properly. You both are working in concert with the mind of Christ; you share one A.I.M. (An Integrated Mind). Because you know that what you have is from God, you show your appreciation by exalting your spouse. The two of you share a last name. "Husbands, love your wives, even as Christ also loved the church, and gave himself for it" (Ephesians 5:25, KJV). In Christ she is W.O.V.E.N.

Acronym to Remember: **W.O.V.E.N.**
(**W**oman/Man **O**f **V**irtue, **E**levated **N**amesake)

Verse to Remember:
"He who finds a wife finds what is good and receives favor from the LORD" (Proverbs 18:22, NIV).

Questions of the Day:
• Have you ever made a bad choice in choosing a date, or even, a mate? If so, what happened?

• When did you begin to see that this person was not right for you?

• Were you the right person at that time?

• How did you err?

• What did your learn from your mistake?

• What insights did you gain from today's reading, and with whom can you share them?

DAY 21

S uccess
M eans
I
L ove
E very day

Figure out what will please Christ, and then do it.

–Ephesians 5:10, The Message

The late Og Mandino, in scroll II of his classic book, *The Greatest Salesman in the World,* said, "I will greet this day with love in my heart, for this is the greatest secret of all success."

When we greet each day with love in our hearts, it puts a smile on God's face. Jesus said, "'Love the Lord your God with all your heart and with all your soul and with all your mind.' This is the first and greatest commandment. And the second is like it: 'Love your neighbor as yourself'" (Matthew 22:37-39, NIV).

Think of a time when you smiled at someone and that person smiled back at you. How did you feel? When others smile back at me, I sometimes feel a connection with them. We can experience that same kind of connection with the Lord. God is love, so reflecting God's love in our actions puts a smile on God's face.

In the morning when I awake, I smile and say, "Good morning, God. What can we create today?" I enter my quiet time, and God puts a smile on my face. God tells me what to write.

Getting to a point in your relationship with God where God speaks to you requires a deeper love for the Lord. God said, "If you love me, show it by doing what I've told you. I will talk to the Father, and he'll provide you another Friend so that you will always have someone with you" (John 14:15, The Message).

The more you study God's Word and live by it, the closer God draws to you. You may find that when you work, you are not working alone; the Holy Spirit is there with you. The Spirit is telling you what to say and what to do so that you might have success (Joshua 1:8).

As we put a smile on God's face, God puts a smile on our faces. As we put a smile on the faces of others, it also puts a bigger smile on both our face and God's. One of the most powerful ways I have found to put a smile on someone's face is to go the extra mile. When I meet others who are striving to move forward in God by doing what God has called them to do, I ask myself and God, "How can we help them?" I include God in the equation because I want to "figure out what will please Christ, and then do it" (Ephesians 5:10, The Message). There are some people God doesn't want you to help, because they have impure agendas.

When God gives me the go-ahead, I look at my assets of value, such as my nationally syndicated radio program, *Power Minutes,* and think of ways I can help assist others. I have done numerous book promotions for others without asking anything in return.

I also assist using third-party assets of value. For example, being syndicated, I have a lot of radio contacts. It's usually as simple as making a phone call to help get someone booked on one of my affiliate stations. When the Holy Spirit leads me to do so, I utilize my third-party assets of value. It puts a big smile on God's face when his children work together, helping one another succeed. This is the true meaning of the second greatest commandment: "Love your neighbor as yourself."

You would help yourself to succeed, wouldn't you? Well, why not help a Christian brother or sister to succeed as well?

Love is the greatest secret to all success. The most successful people I know are all very giving people. They also are very discerning; that's why they are successful. They usually go the extra mile only for those people who are sincere and have the right spirit.

As Solomon wrote in Proverbs,

A generous man will prosper;
he who refreshes others will himself be refreshed.

—Proverbs 11:25, NIV

If you are not receiving much, perhaps it is because you are not giving much. "When you ask, you do not receive, because you ask with the wrong motives" (James 4:3, NIV). God looks into your heart and rewards you according to your love.

Acronym to Remember: S.M.I.L.E.
(Success Means I Love Every day)

Verse to Remember:
"Figure out what will please Christ, and then do it" (Ephesians 5:10, The Message).

Questions of the Day:
• What can you do to demonstrate to God that you love God?

• How can you get closer to God?

• What happens when you draw closer to God?

- What are your assets of value?

- What third-party assets of value do you have access to?

- How can you serve others with your assets?

- What did you learn from today's reading, and with whom can you share it?

The kingdom of
lost-and-found saints

DAY 22

L eaning

O n

S tupid

T hings

… for the Lord disciplines those whom he loves,
and chastises every child whom he accepts.

—Hebrews 12:6, NRSV

It was a hot summer night in 1970 and I was five years old. Outside it was dark. I heard some children yelling the name of a cat. I don't recall the cat's name, but I recognized the voice of the little girl yelling; she was my neighbor Nadine. From the window of an upstairs bedroom, I yelled, "Nadine, what you doin'?"

She replied, "We're looking for our cat." Their cat had strayed away and was lost.

I screamed back, "Wait for me; I'll help you!" I walked downstairs, opened the front door of our house, and left. I was going to help Nadine and her brother look for their cat.

Sometime later, my mother, brother, sister, and several others in the neighborhood were looking for me. To them, I was lost, a five-year-old boy who should have been in bed but was missing from his home in the middle of the night. My mother was terrified.

I heard voices yelling, "Eddie! Eddie!" I recognized one of those voices; it was my mother's.

I yelled back, "Here I am!"

My mother saw me. She didn't say a word but tore off a branch from a tree and walked toward me. At that moment, I knew I was in big trouble. When she got to me, she grabbed my little hand and gave me what's now called an old-fashioned whipping.

When an idea comes to mind, it sometimes seems like the right thing to do. When I heard Nadine's cat was missing, it seemed right to leave the house and help her and her brother find it. However, for me as a child, and one not well informed of all of the dangers lurking outside for unsupervised children, the decision to leave the house was not a decision I had the authority or wisdom to make. With a switch, my mother taught me that lesson that evening.

Just as a young child is to check with a parent and ask, "Is it all right if I go outside?" so we should check with our Father and ask if it's okay to do the things we feel led to do.

When I was in high school, my best friend, Kevin, saved his money from working at McDonalds to buy an old Ford. Kevin really wanted the car, and he wasn't going to let anyone talk him out it. He didn't take his father with him, nor did he ask my dad to look at the car first. He ended up with a lemon. He wasted his time and money. The brakes on the car were worn, and he crashed. He could have lost his life.

In choosing our mates, careers, jobs, and homes, and in making all other major decisions, we must consult the Lord. Without consulting God, we run the risk of experiencing hurt and pain that could have been avoided had we sought God's wisdom.

When we don't consult God, God allows us to make costly mistakes. Through those mistakes, maybe we will learn to seek divine counsel.

If your heart has ever been broken, you've probably asked the same question while drying your tears that I once asked, "Why did God let this happen to me?"

... for the Lord disciplines those whom he loves,
　　and chastises every child whom he accepts.

—Hebrews 12:6, NRSV

God's universe is so orderly that he doesn't have to punish us; we automatically punish ourselves as a result of our not consulting God and his wisdom.

As children, my next-door neighbor Eric and I found a box of what looked like chocolate candy in the bathroom. We didn't ask permission to eat the candy. We just ate the whole box. It turned out to be not candy but Ex-Lax. We both got sick. My dad didn't need to punish us. He supplied us with a toilet and plenty of toilet paper. The punishment took care of itself.

Regardless of our age, in the spiritual realm you and I are like children; there are a lot of things we don't know. We need God's wisdom.

Trust GOD from the bottom of your heart;
    don't try to figure out everything on your own.
Listen for GOD's voice in everything you do, everywhere you go;
    he's the one who will keep you on track.
Don't assume that you know it all.
    Run to GOD!

—Proverbs 3:5-7, The Message

Solomon, author of Proverbs, acknowledged to God that he lacked wisdom. "I am only a little child and do not know how to carry out my duties.... So give your servant a discerning heart to govern your people and to distinguish between right and wrong" (1 Kings 3:7, 9, NIV). He asked for wisdom, and God blessed him with abundant wisdom.

"If any of you lacks wisdom, he should ask God, who gives generously to all without finding fault, and it will be given to him" (James 1:5, NIV). Without wisdom, we lean toward our own limited understanding. When we do this, we foolishly trust our flesh and the things we can see, such as degrees, status, money, possessions, and family name. Consult divine wisdom. A.S.K. G.O.D. (Ask, Seek, Knock; God Opens Doors).

Acronym to Remember: **L.O.S.T.**
(**L**eaning **O**n **S**tupid **T**hings)

Verse to Remember:
"... for the Lord disciplines those whom he loves, and chastises every child whom he accepts" (Hebrews 12:6, NRSV).

Questions of the Day:
• What are some specific instances where you made decisions without consulting God?

• What were the consequences?

• What have you learned from those experiences?

DAY 23

A sk,
S eek,
K nock;

G od
O pens
D oors

Ask, and it shall be given you; seek, and ye shall find; knock, and it shall be opened unto you.

—Matthew 7:7, KJV

You will have complete and free access to God's kingdom, keys to open any and every door: no more barriers between heaven and earth, earth and heaven. A yes on earth is yes in heaven. A no on earth is no in heaven.

—Matthew 16:19, The Message

Recall a time when you were in a difficult situation. Perhaps the things that God was allowing to happen in your life made little sense to you. Where things were heading didn't seem fair. Perhaps your company was downsizing. Your position was eliminated, while others, who seemed to contribute less, kept their jobs. To make matters worse, you were unable to quickly find a job that paid enough to retain the lifestyle you had grown accustomed to. Maybe your problem was completely different. Nevertheless, it was a problem and you didn't know what to do.

Whatever you do, don't give up. Ask God.

The prophet Habakkuk was like many of us. He had some concerns. He didn't like what he was seeing, and he wasn't sure how God would respond.

What's God going to say to my questions? I'm braced for the worst.
    I'll climb to the lookout tower and scan the horizon.
I'll wait to see what God says,
    how he'll answer my complaint.

—Habakkuk 2:1, The Message

When I am troubled, I "climb to the lookout tower" by going to God through H.E.A.R.T. (Higher Empowerment Abides Resourcefully Therein) Meditation™, which you will learn about later.[1] It helps you to scan the horizon of your soul, just as spell check on a computer scans a document and looks for errors, guiding you in making the necessary corrections. Meditation allows you to effectually apply Proverbs 4:23: "Keep thy heart with all diligence; for out of it are the issues of life" (KJV).

When your mind meanders, as it is prone to do, you discipline it by shifting your thoughts and focusing on Jesus. As you train your mind, you can see what kind of thoughts you are thinking. You are able to see that many of your thoughts are often ungodly. As you wait in meditation, you loosen up all the negative baggage that was keeping you from hearing from God. The sin that is in your mind has to be released in order for you to have an effectual prayer life. "We know that God does not listen to sinners" (John 9:31, NIV).

In H.E.A.R.T. (Higher Empowerment Abides Resourcefully Therein) Meditation™, we decrease our thoughts so that we can hear God's answers. As our thoughts decrease, God tells us what to pray for. What God speaks we should write down in our prayer journals.

The prophet Habakkuk listened, as you will learn to do.

GOD answered: "Write this.
    Write what you see.
Write it out in big block letters
    so that it can be read on the run."

—Habakkuk 2:2, The Message

The vision is your prayer. By writing your prayers down, you can read them while you are in pursuit of God's vision for your life.

---

1. *H.E.A.R.T. (Higher Empowerment Abides Resourcefully Therein) Meditation is a registered trademark of Ed Gray.*

> This vision-message is a witness
> pointing to what's coming.
>
> —Habakkuk 2:3, The Message

When God tells you in your meditation to ask for something, you can rest assured that it is coming, provided that you are demonstrating faith by working diligently so that God can bless your works.

One of the things God told Solomon in his meditation is that God would make him wealthy. Solomon's wealth didn't just fall down from the sky. Solomon earned his wealth through shrewd business dealings. Solomon's encounters with God provided wisdom. Wisdom is synonymous with shrewdness. It's an established method of operation based on principles.

Sometimes the things God tells you to pray for seem like they just are not happening. I felt this way about my prayer request to get a publisher for this book. I asked God that the right publisher would sign me. It was a long and arduous process. At times it seemed like it wasn't going to happen. To stay inspired, I reread my vision/prayer and continued working on the book, believing that what I was working on would come to pass. I often read the following:

> It aches for the coming—it can hardly wait!
> And it doesn't lie.
> If it seems slow in coming, wait. It's on its way.
> It will come right on time.
>
> —Habakkuk 2:4, The Message

God delivered on the vision, just as promised.

As you wholeheartedly seek God, the Lord will provide you with divine directives. Before God can bless you with the big things you are asking for, you've got to handle the little things that show up in your meditation, such as the sin God allows you to see as you meditate.

Sometimes in your meditation, cherished sin will show up in your mind, such as desires to commit sexual sin or to eat the wrong foods. Here you are, asking God to bless your work, while you are fantasizing or reflecting about doing something you know in your heart goes against God's Word.

When the sin that is in your heart comes to your awareness, I suggest that you write a prayer of repentance in your journal, acknowledge that you recognize it, and ask God to remove it from your heart. Follow David's example (Psalm 51).

To operate in the higher spiritual realms, you must remove cherished sin. David acknowledged,

If I had cherished sin in my heart,
the Lord would not have listened;
but God has surely listened
and heard my voice in prayer.
Praise be to God,
who has not rejected my prayer
or withheld his love from me!

—Psalm 66:18-20, NIV

God almost always gives you directives on how to bring about what you are praying for. As God speaks ideas to you, write them down in your prayer journal and diligently implement those ideas. The word *knock* in its Hebrew root *daphaq* means "to press severely."[2] The fact is, to make something happen, you have to press severely.

Will you experience rejection from others? Almost certainly! Just because God is with you does not mean that everything is going to be smooth sailing. This truth is evidenced by the experiences of Habakkuk, Moses, Jeremiah, every prophet in the Bible, and, even, our Lord and Savior Jesus Christ. One of the reasons he came to earth is to show us how to overcome obstacles by rising above them. As a saint, A.S.K. (Ask, Seek, and Knock) G.O.D. (God Opens Doors).

Acronym to Remember: **A.S.K. G.O.D.**
(**A**sk, **S**eek, **K**nock; **G**od **O**pens **D**oors)

Verse to Remember:
"Ask, and it shall be given you; seek, and ye shall find; knock, and it shall be opened unto you" (Matthew 7:7, NIV).

---

2. *James Strong*, The Exhaustive Concordance of the Bible *(Madison, N.J.: Published by James Strong, 1890), "Hebrew and Chaldee Dictionary," #1849.*

Questions of the Day:

- What are some specific concerns you have that require an answer from God (finances, career, family, relationships, and so on)?

- Write out specific prayers, asking God to address your specific needs. Expect God to answer.

- When God does answer, write down the answers to your prayers.

DAY 24

S acrifice
A ll
I nner
N egative
T oxins

Be holy; for I am holy.

–Leviticus 11:44, KJV

Paul often referred to the members of the church as saints. Saints are those of us who are striving to live clean lives. God said, "Be holy; for I am holy" (Leviticus 11:44, KJV). A saint is a little god—not God, but one of God's children. "I said, 'You are "gods"; you are all sons of the Most High' " (Psalm 82:6, NIV). As you worship God in spirit and in truth, God purifies your soul and you begin to realize who you are. You stir up the gifts of God that are within you (2 Timothy 1:6).

The word *spirit*, in its original Greek form, *pneuma*, means "air" or "breath."[1] It refers to the soul. "The LORD God formed the man of dust from ground and breathed into his nostrils the breath of life, and man became a living being" (Genesis 2:7, NIV). God blew into each of us special gifts (1 Corinthians 12:7-11).

The Greek form of the word *truth* is *alethes*, meaning "not concealing."[2] When I looked this word up in *Strong's Exhaustive Concordance*, it had the description "a negative particle" in parenthesis. This caused me to ponder, *A negative particle to describe something as positive as truth?*

---

1. *James Strong*, The Exhaustive Concordance of the Bible *(Nashville: Abindgon, 1890)*, "Greek Dictionary of the New Testament," #4151.

2. *James Strong*, The Exhaustive Concordance of the Bible *(Nashville: Abindgon, 1890)*, "Greek Dictionary of the New Testament," #227.

Not everything positive is good.

In my bedroom at home, I have an air purification system called an ionizer. It is designed to rid my physical environment of positive ions. When an atom of oxygen loses an electron, it lacks the negative charge and is therefore positive. This electronless atom is now a positive ion, which is an undesirable condition in your environment. It equals poor air quality that causes irritability, tension, migraines, nausea, and fatigue.

My ionizer negatively charges the ions in the atmosphere, which helps me feel better. Negative ions are oxygen atoms with an extra electron.

Have you ever gone near the ocean or high in the mountains? Do you recall how you felt? It was relaxing, wasn't it?

By the seaside, near waterfalls, and in the mountains are places where thousands of negative ions naturally occur. They create an effect on human biochemistry.

Jesus was obviously aware of this truth. He often went by the water or into the mountains to pray and relax. To worship God in spirit and in truth, we must keep our spiritual air clean. Keeping your spiritual air clean is a lifestyle. It's a way of thinking. As the old saying goes, "Cleanliness is next to godliness." We must position ourselves to think clearly.

For most of my life, Stevie Wonder has been one of my favorite music artists. On his 1995 album *Conversation Peace* there's a song called "Treat Myself," in which he talks about entering a place of beauty and bliss through meditation. In the song, the focus is on Philippians 4:8: "Finally, brothers, whatever is true, whatever is noble, whatever is right, whatever is pure, whatever is lovely, whatever is admirable—if anything is excellent or praiseworthy—think about such things" (NIV). The underlying vocals repeat the verse over and over again.

There have been times in my life when I was in an emotional rut. I was in trouble and didn't know what to do. I closed my eyes and focused on God, and the Lord lifted me out of the emotional rut, which kept my mind intact. As I continued focusing on God, God led me out of my doldrums, which brought about restoration in my life. The Word tells us that God will "provide the way of escape also, so that you will be able to endure it" (1 Corinthians 10:13, NASB). I am a witness of this truth.

Whatever it is that you are going through, God's kingdom within is a bunker of protection where you can go for peace and healing.

Until you begin going inside the kingdom, you will not truly comprehend the meaning of 1 John 4:4: "Greater is He who is in you than he who is in the world" (NASB). He is a healer, a way maker, a provider, a counselor, your Father, and everything you need. Until you truly learn how to go to God, you will continue accepting less than your privilege.

The practice of H.E.A.R.T. (Higher Empowerment Abides Resourcefully Therein) Meditation™ cleanses your spiritual air of toxic thoughts. Just as an ionizer or waterfall adds negative ions that have been lost back into the physical environment, so H.E.A.R.T. (Higher Empowerment Abides Resourcefully Therein) Meditation™ helps replenish the perfect love in your mind that was lost. "Perfect love casts out fear" (1 John 4:18, NASB). God wants you to experience divine love, which is perfect.

When you love someone, you think about him or her. The prophet Isaiah said to God,

> People with their minds set on you,
> > you keep completely whole,
> Steady on their feet.

> —Isaiah 26:3, The Message

As you focus on God, God changes your way of thinking. The Lord changes your life and stabilizes it. The Son leads you to the Father. Jesus said, "I am the way, and the truth, and the life; no one comes to the Father but through Me" (John 14:6, NASB). Jesus is Truth!

As you meditate, focusing on the name of Jesus, you sacrifice all inner toxic thoughts. As you inhale and exhale, you silently focus on the name Jesus. Your exclusive focus on the Christ rids your mental environment of all spiritual toxins.

H.E.A.R.T. (Higher Empowerment Abides Resourcefully Therein) Meditation™, which you will learn in your next reading, is a spiritual air purification system. It is another way of worshiping in spirit and in truth. It helps clear the air in your soul.

When I was a child, my mom used to get upset with me about my messiness. As soon as she'd clean up a room, I'd come in and mess it up again. I believe God feels the same way about us. He will clean the rooms of our minds, and we will entertain the same kinds of toxins that polluted them in the first place: soap operas, raunchy movies, pornography, suggestive music, and conversations that pollute our minds.

The mind is like the body. When the body is not clean, it affects the mind. Likewise, when the mind is not clean, it affects the body. Psychologists have proven that more than 60 percent of all physical illness originates in the mind.

We must put ourselves on better mental diets by being more selective of what we absorb through television, radio, books, the Internet, and especially our conversations. Toxic exposure hinders you from realizing that you are indeed a saint—a child of God.

When toxic chemicals are spilled into the ocean, they kill everything that lives around the spillage, such as fish, sharks, and whales. When you let toxins spill over into your mind, they can kill the saint that lives within you. It causes you and God to spend more time removing toxic waste. Instead, God would prefer to take you to higher heights in the kingdom. God can't lead you into those rooms with a polluted mind. Holiness is required to enter the higher places.

This is what is meant by Jesus' warning, "It is easier for a camel to go through the eye of a needle, than for a rich man to enter into the kingdom of God" (Matthew 19:24, KJV). This does not mean that people with money cannot enter into the kingdom. A rich person with a clean mind can certainly enter, and he or she will become even wealthier. However, if your mind is rich in toxic stuff, you can't enter. God doesn't want that toxic stuff near.

As you draw closer to God, then God will tell you what to remove from your life. If you want to go higher in the kingdom, don't hold on to what God's telling you to let go of. Release it! God can't take you where God wants to lead you if you don't follow divine directives. As Jesus told the disciples, "Anyone who intends to come with me has to let me lead. You're not in the driver's seat; I am" (Matthew 16:24, The Message).

Acronym to Remember: **S.A.I.N.T.**
(**S**piritual **A**ir **I**n the **N**ame of **T**ruth)

Verse to Remember:
"Be holy; for I am holy" (Leviticus 11:44, KJV).

Questions of the Day:
• What does holiness mean to you?

• What is your interpretation of the following verse: "It is easier for a camel to go through the eye of a needle, than for a rich man to enter into the kingdom of God" (Matthew 19:24, KJV)?

• Why is it important to be selective of what you entertain?

- What toxic relationships do you need to end, and why?

- What toxic activities do you need to relinquish?

DAY 25

H igher
E mpowerment
A bides
R esourcefully
T herein

He has planted eternity in the human heart.

—Ecclesiastes 3:11, NLT

If you were attracting things in your life that you did not want, would you want to know how you were doing it? Would you want to know how to stop attracting those things and instead attract what belongs to you by divine right?

Worry is a form of meditation that attracts the things you don't want. Worry is focused thought on something negative. Whatever we focus on we attract. If you focus on sickness or failure, you attract it. As Job said, "What I always feared has happened to me" (Job 3:25, TLB). The devil is like a vicious dog. When he senses your fear, he attacks you at the level of your fear.

When some people think of meditation, they think of it as some New Age, esoteric practice. They conjure up images of putting your mind in neutral and letting it wander. This is the exact opposite of H.E.A.R.T. (Higher Empowerment Abides Resourcefully Therein) Meditation™, which you will be introduced to in this chapter.

If you know how to worry, you already know how to meditate. This lesson is going to teach you how to properly meditate. As you begin a daily practice of H.E.A.R.T. (Higher Empowerment Abides Resourcefully Therein) Meditation™ and prayer, a whole new world will open up to you. You will begin to think clearer thoughts and release stress; your creativity will increase; and you might even experience, as I have, lower blood pressure. My prayer is that you become so focused on God that you become an irresistible magnet, attracting all things that belong to you by divine right.

H.E.A.R.T. (Higher Empowerment Abides Resourcefully Therein) Meditation™ is not complicated. It's doing the same thing you do when you worry, only you focus on Christ instead of your crisis. It provides peace instead of distress.

Meditation is nothing new. It has been in God's family for thousands of years. The first biblical record of someone practicing meditation is found in Genesis. "Isaac went out to meditate in the field at the eventide" (Genesis 24:63, KJV).

Before Jesus taught the disciples how to pray, he told them to do what one does in H.E.A.R.T. (Higher Empowerment Abides Resourcefully Therein) Meditation™. He said, "When you pray, go into your inner room, close your door, and pray to your Father who is in secret, and your Father who sees what is done in secret will reward you" (Matthew 6:6, NASB). The inner room, spiritually speaking, is entered through focused meditation. You have to shut the door to create a vacuum that draws you closer to the secret place.

Here's an old mythical story:

Millions of years ago, shortly after God created the heavens and the earth and everything in it, God and his angels were sitting around and talking. God said to the angels, "I want all of my children to have the key to happiness and success, but I want finding the key to require some effort on their part. Where do you think we should put the key to happiness and success?"

One angel said, "Let's place it on the highest mountain. They'll really have to climb to get it."

God said, "No, that wouldn't be accessible to all of them."

Another angel said, "Let's place it at the bottom of the ocean floor."

God said, "No, that also would be too difficult for some."

A third angel said, "Let's put it inside of them."

God said, "Perfect. Only those who are truly seeking me would ever think of looking there."

The Pharisees, who were the high-ranking religious leaders of that time, demanded of Jesus to know when the kingdom of God should come. Jesus answered, "The kingdom of God does not come with your careful observation, nor will people say, 'Here it is,' or 'There it is,' because the kingdom of God is within you" (Luke 17:20-21, NIV).

During the days of Christ, many religious people had difficulty accepting that the key to all happiness and success was within them. That still holds true today. If I were to say (without referring to Scripture) that the kingdom of God is within you, some people might accuse me of blasphemy. Even when this statement is supported by Scripture, some people still have difficulty accepting that God can be found within us.

You don't have to die to enter the kingdom. Just go inside. H.E.A.R.T. (Higher Empowerment Abides Resourcefully Therein) Meditation™ can help you. Jesus said, "Let not your heart be troubled: ye believe in God, believe also in me. In my Father's house are many mansions: if it were not so, I would have told you. I go to prepare a place for you, I will come again, and receive you unto myself; that where I am, there ye may be also" (John 14:2-3, KJV).

The word *mansion*, in its original Greek form, *skenoo*, means "residence of God." It is a symbol of protection and communion.[1] As we commune with God, we go from one temporary dwelling place to another. "[Because we] continued to behold [in the Word of God] as in a mirror the glory of the Lord, [we] are constantly being transfigured into His very own image in ever increasing splendor and from one degree of glory to another" (2 Corinthians 3:18, The Amplified New Testament). Each time you go into meditation, you access a temporary dwelling place or degree of glory. The more you practice meditation, the more glory you see.

In John 14:1-3 Jesus is saying in effect, "I have gone and prepared a place for you. I will come again and receive you unto myself, that where I am, you may be also."

In one sense, that place is inside you. You access it through daily prayer and meditation. Note also what Jesus said in those verses: "I am going to the Father." In another verse Jesus is quoted as saying, "No one comes to the Father except through me" (John 14:6, NIV).

---

1. *James Strong,* The Exhaustive Concordance of the Bible *(Nashville: Abindgon, 1890),* "Greek Dictionary of the New Testament," #4637.

There are three known dimensions of our minds to which we have access. The first dimension is the conscious mind. That's the state that we operate in when we are consciously aware of what we are doing. For example, through conscious awareness you are reading the pages of this book.

The second dimension is the subconscious mind. I equate this with the mind of Christ referred to in 1 Corinthians 2:16: "But we have the mind of Christ." The subconscious mind is doing trillions of things right now that you are unaware of. It's killing germs, fighting bacteria, regulating the flow of blood, and performing many other key functions that keep you alive and help you to prosper. It's doing these things all at the same time.

The subconscious mind does not differentiate real from imagined. It takes the thoughts that you and I consciously feed it, and it delivers those thoughts to the super consciousness, the Father.

As Jesus indicated, "Whatever you ask in My name, that will I do, so that the Father may be glorified in the Son" (John 14:13, NASB). There's an old saying: "You can't get enough of what you really don't want." Without even being aware of it, many of us are requesting things that we don't want or need in our lives. We are asking for these things through our misdirected meditations. Our negative thoughts are being picked up by our subconscious mind, the mind of Christ, and delivered to the super consciousness, the Father. Those requests are fulfilled and we get exactly what we ask for. We need to clean our minds.

> All of us have become like one who is unclean,
>   and all our righteous acts are like filthy rags.
>
> —Isaiah 64:6, NIV

Each time you meditate, it's like taking a filthy rag and holding it in the middle of a stream of clean water. The water rinses out the dirt.

Often our minds are filled with so much negativity and clutter that we can't hear God. We consciously pray, but we don't feel that our prayers are being answered. Have you ever felt that way?

Prayer is simply talking to God. Meditation is allowing God to talk to you.

God is always communicating with us, but many of us don't hear what God says. One Scripture says, "Many are called, but few are chosen" (Matthew 22:14, KJV). Simply stated, we all are called, but few choose to listen.

As a result of not spending quality time with God, many of us get stuck in ruts. We spend the majority of our lives going to jobs that we hate, because we have not heard what God has called us to do. Many of us are "underemployed," meaning we are doing work that is not in accordance with our highest talents and abilities. As a result, we wake up in the morning saying, "Oh God, it's morning! I have to go to work today" instead of saying, "Good morning, God. What can we create today?"

How do we allow ourselves to get stuck? My friend Omar got up one morning to go to work. He got in his car and tried to start the engine, but it wouldn't start. He thought he needed a boost, so he asked one of his neighbors for a jump.

The neighbor told him to pop the hood. They looked at the battery and saw corrosion around the cables. The neighbor said, "That's your problem. Do you have any soda pop in the house?"

Omar went inside his house and got a can of soda. With a brush and a scraper, they scraped the visible corrosion from the battery and poured some soda on the cables. After cleaning the cables, he was able to start his car.

Sometimes we have corrosion on our souls that makes it difficult for us to connect with God, our power source. The way to clean that corrosion is through prayer and meditation.

When you have a blockage between you and your power source, taking the time to pray is like pouring soda on the wires of your soul. It helps to clean them, and you get a better connection. Meditation is like scraping the corrosion off your soul. It removes some major blockage. God said, "Be still, and know that I am God" (Psalm 46:10, KJV). H.E.A.R.T. (Higher Empowerment Abides Resourcefully Therein) Meditation™ will still your mind so that you can hear God.

When is the best time to meditate? I find the best time for me to meditate is early in the morning. Depending on your schedule, pick a time that you can be alone and undisturbed. "Find a quiet, secluded place so you won't be tempted to role-play before God. Just be there as simply and honestly as you can manage. The focus will shift from you to God, and you will begin to sense his grace" (Matthew 6:6, The Message).

I suggest as a focus word in your meditation the name Jesus. You can also focus on the words like "Jesus Christ" or "Thank you, Jesus." Some other focus words you can use are "Yahweh," "Hosanna," "Emmanuel," or "Abba, Father." You can even use the first few words of your favorite Bible verses, just as long as it is not longer than three words. But again, I highly recommend incorporating the name Jesus in your focus words or just exclusively using the name Jesus as your focus word—the simpler, the better.

How do you use the focus word in your meditation? After you have relaxed your body (as I will show you later), you will inhale deeply, and as you exhale, silently say the name Jesus or any other focus word you have selected for the duration of your meditation. As you begin meditating, you may find it difficult to sit still and be quiet. God obviously knew you'd have difficulty sitting still. That's probably why the Scripture says, "Be still, and know that I am God" (Psalm 46:10, KJV). Don't be alarmed; having difficulty sitting still is normal early in your meditation practice.

Jesus said, "The Comforter, which is the Holy Ghost, whom the Father will send in my name, he shall teach you all things, and bring all things to your remembrance" (John 14:26, KJV). You may notice that thoughts from your childhood will come to mind, and things that you thought you had forgotten will surface. That's normal also. As those thoughts and images come to mind, just let them flow out of you. It's just baggage that needs to be released or important information of which you need reminding. Some of the baggage that you will release may have been holding you back and you didn't even know it was there. Gently return to your focus word and continue meditating.

"Keep thy heart with all diligence; for out of it are the issues of life" (Proverbs 4:23, KJV). Meditation subconsciously causes you to search your own heart. As Jesus said in John 8:32, "You shall know the truth and the truth shall set you free" (personal translation). Many of the unresolved issues that have been holding you back will reveal themselves, and God will work with you in the spiritual realm toward resolving them.

Through the practice of meditation, you will enter a private classroom with God and you will rise to new heights.

As I said earlier, prayer is your talking to God. Meditation is God talking to you. The best time to pray is right after you have meditated. Why? After you have meditated, your heart is in a highly spiritual condition.

You've just communed with God. As the Bible says in Psalm 19:14, "Let the words of my mouth, and the meditation of my heart, be acceptable in thy sight, O LORD, my strength, and my redeemer" (KJV). After you've spent time with God in meditation, the words of your mouth and the meditation of your heart can't help but be acceptable. As a result, the prayers that you pray will be the right prayers. It's almost like taking two electronic components and syncing them together.

Over the years, I have owned several Palm Pilots. Loaded on my desktop computer, I have a Franklin Planner with all my contacts, appointments, my mission statement, and goals. Pretty much all my important information is on my computer. Not unlike yours, my calendar changes by the day.

The same information that I have on my computer I can effortlessly download into the pocket-sized Palm Pilot that I carry with me. I do this by placing my Palm Pilot in its cradle and touching the "Sync" button.

That's what it is like when you connect with God through prayer and meditation. The super conscious mind, through the Holy Spirit, downloads divine ideas and information into your subconscious mind. Prayer and meditation are powerful.

As the Bible says in 1 Corinthians 2:16, "We have the mind of Christ" (NIV). You have access to the mind of Christ when you choose to tap into it. God has been waiting for you. Prayer and meditation form your connection. As the Lord said, "Call to me and I will answer you. I'll tell you marvelous and wondrous things that you could never figure out on your own" (Jeremiah 33:3, The Message). My best work is the result of calling to God through prayer and meditation. God shares insights with me that I could never have figured out on my own. Sometimes God even does it in my sleep. "He gives to His beloved even in his sleep" (Psalm 127:2, NASB).

People who have experienced supernatural success have done so through the simple process of prayer and meditation. Einstein once said, "I want to know the thoughts of God; the rest are details."

I encourage you to meditate twice daily, and immediately following your meditation, go into prayer. Don't worry about what to pray; just pray. Your prayers will be the right prayers.

Meditate twenty to thirty minutes in the morning after you awake, and meditate twenty to thirty minutes again in the afternoon. Go into prayer right after you meditate. Are you ready to meditate?

Meditation Exercise

Sit in a straight-back chair or lie flat on your back in your bed or on the floor, whichever feels the most comfortable to you. Close your eyes. Inhale deeply through your nose. As you exhale, silently count backward from ten with each breath, then relax.

Focus your attention on your feet. Feel your feet getting lighter and lighter, more and more relaxed. Feel this same feeling of looseness, lightness, and relaxation moving upward through your ankles, your calves, and your knees. Feel relaxation moving up your thighs. Feel your buttock muscles relax. Feel your pelvis relax. Relaxation is moving up the lower part of your back, up your spine. Your upper back is relaxed. Relaxation is moving up the lower part of your stomach. Your chest cavity and your chest are relaxed. Your shoulders are relaxed. Relaxation is moving upward through your neck. Your chin is relaxed. Your mouth is relaxed. Your cheeks are relaxed. Your nose, your eyes, and your forehead are relaxed. The top of your head is relaxed. Relaxation is piercing into your deltoids, the sides of your upper arms. Relax. This same feeling of looseness, lightness, and relaxation is moving downward through your triceps, your biceps, your elbows, and your forearms. Your wrists are relaxed. Relaxation is moving downward through your hands, through your fingers, and through the joints of your fingers. All stress is exiting your body now through your fingertips. Relax.

As you exhale, silently repeat your focus word or phrase. As other thoughts come to mind, just dismiss them and gently return to focusing on the name Jesus. Do this for at least twenty minutes. Before awakening from your twenty-minute meditation, count from one to ten and then open your eyes.

For your convenience, I have recorded an audio program called *H.E.A.R.T. (Higher Empowerment Abides Resourcefully Therein) Meditation*™. It will review what you have learned in this chapter and will lead you into meditation without having to remember anything except the name Jesus or your focus word or phrase. You can order a copy at www.edgrayspeaks.com.

After spending time with God in meditation, worship God. I'll speak more on this subject in the next lesson, entitled W.O.R.S.H.I.P. (When Open & Receptive to the Spirit, Healing/Help Is Provided).

Acronym to Remember: **H.E.A.R.T.**
(**H**igher **E**mpowerment **A**bides **R**esourcefully **T**herein)

Verse to Remember:
"The kingdom of God does not come with your careful observation, nor will people say, 'Here it is,' or 'There it is,' because the kingdom of God is within you" (Luke 17:20-21, NIV).

Questions of the Day:
• Where is the kingdom of God?

• In the Bible, who is the first recorded practitioner of meditation?

- According to Matthew 6:6, what did Jesus suggest that the disciples do before praying?

- What are you expecting from the meditation?

- What focus word or phrase will you use in your meditation?

- What are the times you have scheduled to meditate?

DAY 26

W hen
O pen &
R eceptive to the
S pirit,
H ealing/Help
I s
P rovided

Give unto the LORD the glory due unto his name; worship the Lord in the beauty of holiness.

—Psalm 29:2, KJV

My question: What are God-worshipers like?
Your answer: Arrows aimed at God's bull's-eye.

—Psalm 25:12, The Message

You and I were made to worship God. The first commandment given to humankind was to worship (Exodus 20:1-6). When Jesus taught his disciples to pray, he told them to worship before making their requests to God.

> Pray, then, in this way:
> "Our Father who is in heaven,
> Hallowed be Your name."

—Matthew 6:9, NASB

Worship is taking the spotlight off of you and acknowledging who God is. God is your Creator, and even his name is holy.

You cannot come into the presence of God without experiencing change. Solomon went up to a high place to worship and sacrifice unto God.

That night, there in Gibeon, GOD appeared to Solomon in a dream: God said, "What can I give you? Ask."

Solomon said, "You were extravagantly generous in love with David my father, and he lived faithfully in your presence, his relationships were just and his heart was right. And you have persisted in this great and generous love by giving him—and this very day!—a son to sit on his throne.

"And now here I am: GOD, my God, you have made me, your servant, ruler of the kingdom in place of David my father. I'm too young for this, a mere child! I don't know the ropes, I hardly know the 'ins' and 'outs' of this job. And here I am, set down in the middle of the people you've chosen, a great people—far too many to ever count.

"Here's what I want: Give me a God-listening heart so I can lead your people well, discerning the difference between good and evil. For who on their own is capable of leading your glorious people?"

God, the Master, was delighted with Solomon's response. And God said to him, "Because you have asked for this and haven't grasped after a long life, or riches, or doom of your enemies, but you have asked for the ability to lead and govern well, I'll give you what you've asked for—I'm giving you a wise and mature heart. There's never been one like you before; and there'll be no one after. As a bonus, I'm giving you both the wealth and glory you didn't ask for—there's not a king anywhere who will come up to your mark."

—1 Kings 3:5-14, The Message

"God is a Spirit: and they that worship him must worship him in spirit and in truth" (John 4:24, KJV). To worship God in spirit requires going to a high place in your own spirit, rising above your circumstances and seeking the face of God, as did Solomon.

"The king went to Gibeon to offer sacrifices, for that was the most important high place" (1 Kings 3:4, NIV). Gibeon, translated, means "high place."

The most important high place to which you and I can go to make sacrifice is in our souls. This is what Jesus meant when he said, "When you pray, go into your [most] private room, and, closing the door, pray to your Father, Who is in secret; and your Father, Who sees in secret, will reward you in the open" (Matthew 6:6, The Amplified New Testament). You have to get inside yourself in order to enter the high place. We are instructed to close the door, because you cannot arrive at the high place by focusing on anything but God.

To get to the high place in our souls, we have to let go of all our attachments to F.A.L.S.E. G.O.D.S. (Fear/Fornication, Anger/Adultery, Laziness/Lasciviousness, Sloth, Envy, Greed/Guilt, Overindulgence, Despair, and Sin). We have to close the door on everything except God. The kingdom within is a holy place; anything that is unholy is not authorized to enter. God said, "Thou shalt have no other gods before me" (Exodus 20:3, KJV). If we are carrying untruth, we cannot arrive at the high place within ourselves where God dwells.

Worship requires surrender. It is almost impossible to surrender to God if you don't trust God. J.E.S.U.S. (Jesus' Example Shows Ultimate Surrender) was completely surrendered to God. He said only what God told him to say, and he did everything out of this relationship and understanding (John 12:49). The night before the Crucifixion, he uttered these words: "My Father, if it is possible, may this cup be taken from me. Yet not as I will, but as you will" (Matthew 26:39, NIV).

Surrendering often means doing things you don't feel like doing. Since we come to our faith in God through a relationship with Christ, we are to surrender to Jesus just as he did to God, even when we don't feel like it. "If anyone wishes to come after Me, he must deny himself, and take up his cross daily and follow Me" (Luke 9:23, NASB). This means to pray, meditate, read the Bible, and obey the Word even when you don't feel like it.

Jesus is truth. To worship God in spirit and in truth means to focus on Jesus, sacrifice all thoughts that are not like his, and submit to the Spirit. True worship brings us into the presence of God, where healing and help are provided. God provides the instructions we need to handle our exact circumstances, just as God did for Solomon, who needed wisdom to better perform his job as king.

To my knowledge, every person in the Bible who came to Jesus with a request for healing and whose requests were granted came to him first in worship. For example,

A man with leprosy came and knelt before him and said, "Lord, if you are willing, you can make me clean."

Jesus reached out his hand and touched the man. "I am willing," he said. "Be clean!" Immediately he was cured of his leprosy.

—Matthew 8:2-3, NIV

The fact that he knelt before Jesus is symbolic of his worship.

If your prayers are not being answered, check to see if you have been worshiping God in spirit and in truth. Worshiping God is A.W.E.S.O.M.E. (As We Experience Spirit, Our Minds Expand).

Acronym to Remember: **W.O.R.S.H.I.P.**
(**W**hen **O**pen & **R**eceptive **T**o the **S**pirit, **H**ealing/Help **I**s **P**rovided)

Verse to Remember:
"God is a Spirit: and they that worship him worship him in spirit and in truth" (John 4:24, KJV).

Questions of the Day:
• Why were you made?

• How does God expect us to worship?

• What does it mean to worship in spirit and in truth?

• What did the man with leprosy in Matthew 8:2-3 do that got Jesus' attention?

• What are you doing to get God's attention?

• What are your patterns of worship?

DAY 27

A s
W e
E xperience
S pirit,
O ur
M inds
E xpand

Delight yourself in the LORD;
and He will give you the desires of your heart.

—Psalm 37:4, NASB

"God formed Man out of dirt from the ground and blew into his nostrils the breath of life. The Man came alive—a living soul!" (Genesis 2:7, The Message). Spirit is what God breathed into the man. Although the Spirit of God is within those of us who have accepted Christ, many Christians do not experience God's presence in their lives. Since they lack true belief, they dare not think that the Spirit of God could possibly dwell within them. "'If you can'?" said Jesus. "Everything is possible for him who believes" (Mark 9:23, NIV). This includes experiencing the presence of God in your life. If you are one who professes to be a believer, but in your heart you know you are not, confess to Jesus, "I do believe; help me overcome my unbelief!" (Mark 9:24, NIV).

To "delight," in the original context of Psalm 37:4, means to "luxuriate." To luxuriate is to grow with vigor and in great abundance. As you luxuriate yourself in God, your mind cannot help but expand. A mind stretched by the awesomeness of God leaves lack and limitation behind and can never regain its previous limited dimension.

When your mind is stretched, your possibilities expand. You affirm, "I can do all things through Christ which strengtheneth me" (Philippians

144

4:13, KJV). Christ is the Spirit inside you. You are capable of all things that he has ordained for you to do. "For as he thinketh in his heart, so is he" (Proverbs 23:7, KJV). The "heart" here refers to the root of your mind, known as the soul.

David delighted himself in the Lord and walked according to God's statutes. God remained with David and provided him with wisdom, strength, power, protection, and wealth. His son Solomon in his youth delighted in the Lord. God likewise provided Solomon with wisdom and all the desires of his heart.

Stay focused and let God's focus increase in you. When God supplies you, he surprises you. Solomon delighted himself in the Lord. It led him to sacrifice at Gibeon, which means "high place." When you meditate, focusing on God, you are going to some of the highest heights that you rise to. "In Gibeon the LORD appeared to Solomon in a dream at night, and God said, 'Ask what you wish me to give you'" (1 Kings 3:5, NASB).

Solomon asked for wisdom, but God surprised him. God gave him what he asked for and in addition gave him riches and honor unequal to those of any other person during his time. God also told Solomon, "'If you will walk in my ways and obey my statutes and commands as David your father did, I will give you a long life.' Then Solomon awoke—and he realized it had been a dream" (1 Kings 3:14, NIV).

The dreams of those who delight in the Lord do indeed come true. You cannot see your full possibilities in the natural. It is beyond your comprehension (Luke 17:20-21). Delighting in the Lord helps you to see possibilities that are impossible to comprehend in your carnal mind. The poet Robert Browning understood this when he wrote,

Ah, but a man's reach should exceed his grasp,
Or what's a heaven for?

It is all within your G.R.A.S.P. (God Rewards All Serious/Seeking Persons).

Men and women will not strive or even ask of God beyond what they think God will give them. Those who believe Paul's promise that "God will meet all your needs according to his glorious riches in Christ Jesus" (Philippians 4:19, NIV) will believe that the things God shows them in their dreams, regardless of their present situation or the extravagance of their vision, are possible.

When you delight in the Lord, the Lord stretches your vision. God causes you to see beyond your painful past. "Arise [from the depression and prostration in which circumstances have kept you—rise to a new life]! Shine (be radiant with the glory of the Lord), for your light has come, and the glory of the Lord is risen upon you!" (Isaiah 60:1, Amplified Bible, Old Testament).

Jabez was a child who was born in pain. God caused him to rise above the pain. "Jabez was more honorable than his brothers" (1 Chronicles 4:9, NIV). He delighted himself in the Lord. "Jabez cried out to the God of Israel, 'Oh, that you would bless me and enlarge my territory! Let your hand be with me, and keep me from harm so that I will be free from pain.' And God granted his request" (1 Chronicles 4:10, NIV). God can do the same for you.

I encourage you to luxuriate in the presence of God. Meditate, pray, study the Word day and night, listen to audio programs, learn from presentations, and read books such as this one. Act upon what God shows you and share your experiences with others. God will lift you out of your pain, and you will see for yourself that God is A.W.E.S.O.M.E. (As We Experience Spirit, Our Minds Expand), and our territories expand, too.

Acronym to Remember: **A.W.E.S.O.M.E.**
(**A**s **W**e **E**xperience **S**pirit, **O**ur **M**inds **E**xpand)

Verse to Remember:
"Delight yourself in the LORD; and He will give you the desires of your heart" (Psalm 37:4, NASB).

Questions of the Day:
• How can you delight yourself in the Lord?

- Why is focus on God so important?

- How does delighting in the Lord assist you?

DAY 28

S eek an
E ver
C loser
R elationship;
E nlightening
T ruths may follow

Unto you it is given to know the mystery of the kingdom of God.

—Mark 4:11, KJV

The secrets of the kingdom were esoteric to most people, including religious people during the time of Christ. Not much has changed. Although God wants all of us to enter the kingdom, not all will be selected for admission. "For many are called, but few are chosen" (Matthew 22:14, KJV).

Why is that? Not everyone has an interest in a personal relationship with God through Jesus Christ. God, through Christ, reserves enlightenment for those who are truly seeking enlightenment through a personal relationship with the Lord. This is accomplished by letting go of attitudes that cause T.E.A.R.S. (Traditional Entrapment/Ecclesiastical Apartheid Restricting Spirit). The Pharisees missed the secrets of the kingdom because they were locked into tradition.

Apartheid was policy in the Republic of South Africa up until the 1990s. Negroes and other people of black descent were segregated and discriminated against in spite of the fact that they, too, are God's creations. We do the same thing spiritually. Jesus spoke the truth in a manner that was much different from the traditional teachings, and he was attacked for it. It is not that he preached a false doctrine. He spoke the truth that was based upon his opponents' own Scriptures. However, he illuminated what they were unable to see and unwilling to receive.

Only those whose hearts were open and receptive to the voice of God received his enlightenment. The disciples came to him and asked him why he spoke to people in parables. He replied,

The knowledge of the secrets of the kingdom of heaven has been given to you, but not to them....

Though seeing, they do not see;

though hearing, they do not hear or understand.

In them is fulfilled the prophecy of Isaiah:

You will be ever hearing but never understanding;

you will be ever seeing but never perceiving.

For this people's heart has become calloused;

they hardly hear with their ears,

and they have closed their eyes.

Otherwise they might see with their eyes,

hear with their ears,

understand with their hearts

and turn, and I would heal them.

—Matthew 13:11-15, NIV

Sometimes we can become so trapped in religiosity that we miss revelation and illumination when they are presented to us. To receive illumination, you must love Christ and have a personal relationship with him.

Dr. George Washington Carver was perhaps the most prolific agricultural scientist of all time. In the early 1900s Carver invented more than 300 uses for peanuts, including peanut butter. Carver did not patent peanut butter, as he believed food products were all a gift from God.

Dr. Carver was the head of the agricultural department at Tuskeegee Institute, an agricultural college for blacks. In addition to educating students, Dr. Carver taught more productive agricultural practices to Southern farmers. After finding so many uses for peanuts, Carver lectured about their use before a committee of Congress. He received many awards such as the Spingarn Medal from the National Association for the Advancement of Colored People and the Theodore Roosevelt Medal for his valuable contributions to science. There is a George Washington Carver National Monument on the Missouri farm where Carver was born, and January 5 has been named George Washington Carver Day.

An older minister whom I met in Detroit, Dr. Phillip Lenuud, heard Dr. Carver speak many years ago at a church pastored by Lenuud's dad. Dr. Carver told a story of his friendship with Henry Ford. According to the story, Henry Ford came down to Tuskegee Institute, Alabama, to visit Dr. Carver and discuss a problem.

Ford said, "George, I need your help. People are being killed in my cars. When accidents occur and the windshields break, the glass sometimes cuts their throats."

Carver said, "All right, Henry, I'll ask God." Carver was confident that God would provide an answer, just as God had done in leading Carver to his other inventions.

As Henry Ford was leaving, he asked Carver, "How is it that you are able to make so much out of peanuts?"

Carver answered, "When you love something enough, it reveals itself to you." Dr. Carver loved peanuts. God did the same thing with Moses and his wooden staff. Moses was once a shepherd. He was very familiar with using a staff.

When we love the Word of God, God reveals himself to us through the Word. "The secret things belong to the LORD our God, but the things revealed belong to us and to our children forever, that we may follow all the words of this law" (Deuteronomy 29:29, NIV).

I believe that the closer you get in relationship with God, the more God will reveal things to you. There were things Jesus shared with the seventy disciples in his outer circle that he did not share with the masses. However, he shared those same things and much more with the twelve who were in his inner circle. Peter, James, and John were in his close circle. He shared the same insights with them that he shared with the seventy and the twelve. However, he revealed much more to them than he did to all the others.

Success in the kingdom is based on relationship. Seek a closer personal relationship with Christ, and he will reveal the S.E.C.R.E.T. (Seek an Ever Closer Relationship; Enlightening Truths may follow). Tell God of your desire to draw closer. Tell God you want to be a close and dear friend. "Come near to God and he will come near to you" (James 4:8, NIV).

Acronym to Remember: S.E.C.R.E.T.
(**S.E.C.R.E.T.** (**S**eek an **E**ver **C**loser **R**elationship;
Enlightening **T**ruths may follow)

Verse to Remember:
"Unto you it is given to know the mystery of the kingdom of God"
(Mark 4:11, KJV).

Questions of the Day:
• How close to God do you want to be? Why?

• Based upon what you have learned over the past several days, what are some things you can do to draw closer to God?

• What will it cost you?

• Are you willing to pay the price?

151

- In addition to what you have learned these past several days, what are some other things that you know are required for you to draw closer to God?

- Are you already doing these things?

- If not, what has stopped you?

Spiritual
politics

DAY 29

L ife
I s
M easured
I n
T hought

Be careful how you think; your life is shaped by your thoughts.

—Proverbs 4:23, TEV

The life you live, whether good or bad, you created. It was first created in your mind based on your thoughts. Those thoughts transformed into attitudes and beliefs, from which you spoke and acted accordingly.

If you are unhappy and not prosperous, it's not God's fault. God made you in the divine image and likeness, and God gave you power. Because you lacked knowledge of who you are and the power you have in Christ, you might have unknowingly used that power against yourself.

The good news is that you have the power to change your circumstances through Christ our Lord. If it is possible for others, such as Oprah Winfrey, to rise from a life of poverty and abuse to a life of serving others, it is possible for you. If it is possible for a factory worker in Detroit named Barry Gordy to rise from obscurity to creating a musical legacy named Motown, it is possible for you. If it is possible in the world, it is possible in you; you only need to figure out how.

God told Jeremiah, "I know the plans I have for you, plans to prosper you and not to harm you, plans to give you hope and a future" (Jeremiah 29:11, NIV). Doing those things that please God reveals God's plan for you. "Figure out what will please Christ, and then do it" (Ephesians 5:8, The Message). God's Word, meditation, prayer, and experience will show you. The Lord said, "The things you don't allow on earth will be the things that God does not allow, and the things you allow on earth will be the things that God allows" (Matthew 16:19, NCV).

The earth represents the world that you and I physically live in. Heaven represents our souls (Luke 17:20-22). Many of us have limited or shut off our blessings through our limited thinking. We have placed a limit on ourselves as to what is possible for us. Even though we believe in God, we cannot pray beyond our faith.

Earl Graves is a figure of international renown in the African American community. His accomplishments are many. In addition to being the publisher of *Black Enterprises* magazine, Graves has many other successful business ventures that include several Pepsi bottling franchises in the U. S. and South Africa. Graves has served on the boards of Aetna Life and Casualty Company, American Airlines, Chrysler Corporation, Federated Department Stores, Inc., and Rohmn and Haas Corporation. A few years ago, I was privileged to host a chat room discussion with Earl Graves for my *Power Minute* listening audience. Graves said, "If I had shared these possibilities with my college classmates, they would have laughed at me."

Graves's belief system is what made it possible. "According to your faith be it unto you" (Matthew 9:29, KJV). Contrary to what a lot of people believe, God did not exclude any ethnic group from prosperity. On the contrary, God reserved abundance for every member of the human race who believes. "'If you can'? said Jesus. 'Everything is possible for him who believes'" (Mark 9:23, NIV).

You can! If it is possible for others, it is possible for you; you only need to know how. So that you will understand, let's go back to the beginning of creation to gain an understanding of how God works.

"In the beginning God created the heavens and the earth. Now the earth was formless and empty, darkness was over the surface of the deep, and the Spirit of God was hovering over the waters" (Genesis 1:1, NIV).

In the beginning, there was nothing. In your life, you might feel that you have nothing. You might be without a job or even a home. Your spouse might have left you for someone else. You might feel as if a dark cloud is hovering over like darkness over the earth in the beginning. Fear not, for God is with you (Isaiah 41:13). The Spirit is within you as the Spirit was hovering over the waters. With the Spirit's help, you are about to embark upon the creation of a lifetime by following God's examples, which are being imparted to you.

On day one, God created light. Preceding the account of that creation are three words: "And God said" (Genesis 1:3).

On day two, God created the sky, land, and sea. Preceding the story of those creations are three words: "And God said" (Genesis 1:6,9).

On day three, God created vegetation. Preceding the story of that creation are three words: "Then God said" (Genesis 1:11).

On day four, God created the sun and the moon. Preceding that story are three words: "And God said" (Genesis 1:14).

On day five, God made the water teem with living creatures. Preceding the account of that creation are three words: "And God said" (Genesis 1:20).

Finally, on day six, God created humankind. "Then God said, 'Let us make man in our image, in our likeness'" (Genesis 1:26).

What comes before any spoken word? A thought does. You first think it. Your thoughts are the origins of the words you speak. That is why Jesus said, "... it is not what goes into the mouth that defiles a person, but it is what comes out of the mouth that defiles" (Matthew 15:11, NRSV). And, he continued, "... what comes out of the mouth proceeds from the heart, and this is what defiles" (Matthew 15:18, NRSV).

Your thoughts are at the root of your heart. Therefore,

Above all else, guard your heart,
for it is the wellspring of life.

—Proverbs 4:23, NIV

Whatever you think, that's what is going to expand. If you think lack and limitation, then lack and limitation will grow in your life. If you think, *There is no lack and limitation in God's kingdom, and I believe that I can do all things through Christ who strengthens me,* then possibilities will expand in your life. You will think a thought, then speak it, and God will lead you through the manifestation. You will discover that you have C.L.O.U.T. (Christ Loves Our Unlimited Thinking).

Acronym to Remember: **L.I.M.I.T.**
(**L**ife **I**s **M**easured **I**n **T**hought)

Verse to Remember:
"Be careful how you think; your life is shaped by your thoughts" (Proverbs 4:23, TEV).

Questions of the Day:
- Read Matthew 16:17. Have the thoughts you have been loosening on earth been of positive possibilities or have they been thoughts of failure?

- If those thoughts are received in heaven, what do you think is happening?

- Read Mark 9:23, and describe the importance of belief.

- What three words did God speak before he created? (See Genesis 1:3,6,9,11,14,20,26.)

- What comes before any spoken word?

- What thoughts do you have about yourself and your future that you need to change?

DAY 30

C hrist
L oves
O ur
U nlimited
T hinking

God . . . calleth those things which be not as though they were.

—Romans 4:17, KJV

The word *confess* means "to speak or manifest." Prior to God's confessing, "Let there be," the earth "was without form, and void; and darkness was upon the face of the deep" (Genesis 1:2, KJV). The Spirit of the Lord moved. The Creator called forth things that were not as though they were, then manifested them. God didn't just talk the talk. God followed it up with action and manifested divine thought. You and I have that same kind of power, for we are made in the image and likeness of God (Genesis 1:26). "I have said, Ye are gods; and all of you are children of the most High" (Psalm 82:6, KJV).

"Greater is he that is within you, than he that is within the world" (1 John 4:4, KJV). The realization of this truth occurs when you recognize the power you have in Christ. Paul recognized this power when he said, "I pray that you may be active in sharing your faith, so that you will have a full understanding of every good thing we have in Christ" (Philemon 6, NIV). As I share what God has revealed to me, my understanding increases.

During the writing of this book, I envisioned you and many others reading and sharing the insights with others. I saw God moving through these pages and healing many souls.

Write the vision,
And make it plain on tablets,
That he may run who reads it.

159

For the vision is yet for an appointed time;
But at the end it will speak, and it will not lie.
Though it tarries, wait for it;
Because it will surely come,
it will not tarry.

—Habakkuk 2:2-3, NKJV

I wrote my vision down, and I believed it.

My belief is the result of knowing God, not myself. "For mortals it is impossible, but for God all things are possible" (Matthew 19:26, NRSV). I know that I am not writing this book; God is writing it through me. I know that greater is Christ who is within me than the devil who is within the world. I know that God lives within me to the extent that God's Word lives in me. As I write and as I speak, I am simply manifesting the Word. God's Word does not return void. I also know that God loves unlimited thinking! Jesus did not think in terms of limits. He said, "All things can be done for the one who believes" (Mark 9:23, NRSV).

As you operate in your gift under the guidance of the Holy Spirit, and as you do the assignment that God has ordained you to complete, your success will be extraordinary. How do I know this? Jesus said so. "I tell you the truth, anyone who has faith in me will do what I have been doing. He will do even greater things than these, because I am going to the Father. And I will do whatever you ask in my name, so that the Son may bring glory to the Father" (John 14:12-13, NIV). Christ adds super to your natural and produces supernatural results.

When you are faithfully operating in your calling, thinking and speaking correctly and living right, the Son assists you in achieving extraordinary success. This glorifies God.

God hates limited thinking. To place a limit on God is insulting to God and demonstrates a lack of faith. "Without faith it is impossible to please him" (Hebrews 11:6, KJV). You cannot serve a big God and think small. If you believe in Jesus, abide in God's Word and seek God's help, you will discover that you have C.L.O.U.T. (Christ Loves Our Unlimited Thinking).

Acronym to Remember: C.L.O.U.T.
(Christ Loves Our Unlimited Thinking)

Verse to Remember:
"God ... calleth those things which be not as though they were" (Romans 4:17, KJV).

Questions of the Day:
• Define the word *confess*.

• Write out Psalm 82:6.

• Do you truly believe what God says in Psalm 82:6?

• Write out Hebrews 11:6.

- Read John 14:12-13. What does this Scripture mean to you?

- Do you believe you have C.L.O.U.T.?

DAY 31

P ower
O f
L ife
I s in the
T ongue;
I t
C reates &
A ffirms
L ife

Moderation is better than muscle,
self-control better than political power.

—Proverbs 16:32, The Message

One of the Ten Commandments says, "You shall not murder" (Exodus 20:13, NIV). Killing is prevalent in our society. Spiritual murder is the most devastating form. Earthly lawmakers permit it and even use it against themselves to get elected. Political ad campaigns assassinate the character of opponents while embellishing the records of the candidate whose campaign is paying for the ad.

Divorce is prevalent in our society. Character assassination is normal in divorce cases, especially when there are assets to divide. Sometimes Christians take on a personality that is very different from that of Christ. Under oath and under stress, they might take on an entirely different character. Some say whatever is necessary to serve themselves without getting caught. In the worst cases, they embellish, lie, deny, and attack. It's not about serving truth; it's about getting or keeping stuff.

Killing is prevalent in many of our churches. I didn't realize how political the church could be until many years ago when I became active in behind-the-scenes processes at the church. I was so disappointed at how cutthroat some people can be that I almost gave up on church.

My pastor gave me spiritual mouth-to-mouth resuscitation by counseling me. He helped me to see that church organizations are not always the church organism. Individuals who live and operate in accordance with God's spiritual system individually and collectively are the real church. The legitimate church operates in faith, while the illegitimate church operates by what it sees. It sometimes sees money as the source of its dreams and blind ambitions. The self-serving church professes, "In God we trust," but it really believes in money. It uses fear, intimidation, and embellishment to extract resources and talents from others.

As the legitimate church, "we live by faith, not by sight" (2 Corinthians 5:7, NIV). You cannot function well in both systems. To do so would be like a business having two sets of books, one that has legitimate profits and losses and another that deceptively hides the losses while inflating the profits. The book with the losses is shown to unsavvy employees to "rational-lie" not paying their justly deserved bonuses. The book with the profits is shown to Wall Street and the shareholders to inflate the value of the stock. The only people who profit are the people behind the scheme.

"No one can serve two masters. Either he will hate the one and love the other, or he will be devoted to the one and despise the other. You cannot serve both God and Money" (Matthew 6:24, NIV). However, you can serve God and then money will serve you. God is the source of everything you need and want. "Seek first the kingdom of God and His righteousness, and all these things shall be added to you" (Matthew 6:33, NKJV).

Just as God has a kingdom, so does Satan. God's politics and Satan's politics are very different. The politics of the kingdom of God is righteousness. A true believer operates in a manner that would allow him or her to remain prosperous and in right standing with God. Such a believer does not seek to control but rather to be governed by the Holy Spirit. As leaders, this person seeks (as did Solomon) godly wisdom to better govern God's people.

Politics is the science of getting things done. Satan uses intrigue and deception, control and manipulation in his strategies to obtain control. These things are spiritually illegal.

Now the works of the flesh are manifest, which are these; Adultery, fornication, uncleanness, lasciviousness, idolatry, witchcraft, hatred, variance, emulations, wrath, strife, seditions, heresies, envying, murders, drunkenness, revellings, and such like: of the which I tell you before, as I have also told you in time past, that they which do such things shall not inherit the kingdom of God.

—Galatians 5:19-21, KJV

Divine spiritual politics are quite different. This system does not use deception, accusation, control, or manipulation to produce results. Its arsenal is the fruit of the Spirit. "The fruit of the Spirit is love, joy, peace, longsuffering, gentleness, goodness, faith, meekness, temperance: against such there is no law" (Galatians 5:22-23, KJV).

None of the weapons in Satan's negative arsenal can match your weapons. When you rely upon the fruit of the Spirit,

No weapon forged against you will prevail,

and you will refute every tongue that accuses you.

—Isaiah 54:17, NIV

You cannot use Satan's arsenal and manipulate, lie, cheat, steal, or kill your way into God's kingdom of love. That would be like pouring kerosene, which looks and smells like gas, in your gas tank and thinking that it will work!

You are a Christlike being. Christlike beings operate under a different system. Your power comes from the Holy Spirit and is provided by the fruit of the Spirit. Everything you need to produce results is in the fruit of the Spirit; you just need to become proficient in using them.

Love

Begin to practice love! "Love thy neighbour as thyself" (Leviticus 19:18, KJV). Jesus said we are to "love one another as I have loved you" (John 15:12, NRSV). Sometimes love can be an arduous task, especially when others have hurt, used, or abused you. However, we must practice love in order to produce godly fruit. Love does not mean you always have to be around those who hate you. You can love them at a distance! "Love your enemies, bless them that curse you, do good to them that hate you, and pray for them which despitefully use you, and persecute you" (Matthew 5:44, KJV). Pray for them and send them love.

Joy

Find joy! Joy is not just about feeling happy or walking around with a smile on your face. Phony joy is not real.

I have seen people buy 3 series BMWs or 300 series Mercedes and change the decals so that it appears as if they have the more expensive and powerful car. They replace the 3 series BMW logo with the more prestigious M3 logo, or they replace the 300 series Mercedes logo with the more prestigious 500. They are able to fool those not familiar with the cars, but they can't fool themselves or those who are knowledgeable.

Likewise, we can fool others with phony joy, but we are not able to fool God or ourselves. God knows you are hurting and weak, and you know it. Real joy is the result of facing your weakness and asking God to cleanse you of all unrighteousness. After David sinned with Bathsheba, he repented. He went to God and acknowledged his fault. He said,

Against you, you only, have I sinned
and done what is evil in your sight.

—Psalm 51:4, NIV

He also acknowledged what God wants from us:
You desire truth in the inner parts;
you teach me wisdom in the inmost place.

—Psalm 51:6, NIV

He then asked God to cleanse him.

As human beings operating in a nonspiritual system, we sometimes are more concerned about how we appear on the outside—our appearance and image. God is more concerned about our inside.

Until you can truly acknowledge your weakness and faults on the inside and confess them to God, you will never find joy. Joy is a willful choice. It requires open and honest discourse with God and yourself. As Jesus said, "Behold, the kingdom of God is within you" (Luke 17:21, KJV). Even though it is within, you have to be honest with yourself and God to enter.

Peace

David didn't just acknowledge his wrong; he rose above it. He told God, "Then will I teach transgressors thy ways; and sinners shall be converted unto thee" (Psalm 51:13, KJV). This sinner (David) taught us God's ways through his many psalms. The best preachers and teachers are reformed sinners. They have testimonies.

Whatever God delivers you from, go back and help others who are struggling with the same thing. You are in an excellent position to help them. You understand their pain because you have been there. Find peace within. Peace does not come from outside you.

A few years ago, when my money evaporated and my heart was broken, I still found peace. I didn't wait for my prosperity to be restored. I didn't look for a relationship to make me happy. Instead, I looked up to Christ, and I found peace. Peace is God's promise when you focus on God. "Thou wilt keep him in perfect peace, whose mind is stayed on thee: because he trusteth in thee" (Isaiah 26:3, KJV).

When I was going through my heartbreak, was I tempted to look for a quick fix to fulfill my needs? Yes. Was I tempted to slip into depression? Yes. But I flipped the script and pursued the Spirit with great intensity.

Claiming peace, which you have in your arsenal, will allow you to get through any circumstance. Its power is beyond explanation. "The peace of God, which passeth all understanding, shall keep your hearts and minds through Christ Jesus" (Philippians 4:7, KJV).

Longsuffering

Longsuffering will lead you to a breakthrough. *Longsuffering* is an old English word that means "patience." Call upon your faith. Follow the Holy Spirit's directives and just believe. "All things can be done for the one who believes" (Mark 9:23, NRSV).

Whatever it is that you are going through, God is allowing you to go through it for a reason. God is preparing you for something greater. As James said, "Consider it pure joy, my brothers, whenever you face trials of many kinds, because you know that the testing of your faith develops perseverance. Perseverance must finish its work so that you may mature and complete, not lacking anything" (James 1:2-4, NIV). Don't slip into temptation, whatever it may be. Use your weapon of patience and wait for your breakthrough!

Gentleness

Operating in the Christlike political system also requires proficiency in the weapon of gentleness. You have to be gentle with yourself and gentle with others, even when they are fighting you. Your gentleness keeps you from saying or doing the wrong thing. It allows you to operate in wisdom. We have to understand that the enemy uses people who are near and dear to us to get us to respond in ways that damage our Christian witness and bring shame to God. These individuals are not our real enemies; Satan is. We are *in* the world but not *of* it. Therefore, we don't have to fight with the same weapons of Satan's kingdom. "Behold," said Jesus, "I send you forth as sheep in the midst of wolves: be ye therefore wise as serpents, and harmless as doves" (Matthew 10:16, KJV).

Lena Horn said in the classic movie *Cabin in the Sky,* "Sometimes you got to beat the devil at his own game." You beat him by not using the weapons that he designed and mastered but by using your own weapons. Gentleness is a weapon that you want to master. There's an old saying: "You catch more flies with honey than you do with vinegar."

Goodness

To operate in the correct political system, we must also practice goodness. Strive to be in right standing with God by doing the things God tells you to do. Stand on the Word. I don't know about you, but every time I do what my flesh tells me to do, I err and get spiritually beat up. If you haven't realized this yet, that is because your errors have not yet caught up with you.

Faith

The spiritual political system requires faith. Faith is not just a matter of belief. Faith is a matter of action. You won't act in accordance with principles in which you don't believe. If you do not trust in God, these principles that are being shared will not work for you. "Faith without works is dead" (James 2:20, KJV).

Meekness

The spiritual political system requires meekness. Meekness is humility. "Live creatively, friends. If someone falls into sin, forgivingly restore him, saving your critical comments for yourself. *You* might be needing forgiveness before the day's out" (Galatians 6:1, The Message). In recent years we have seen ministers and politicians murder the character of others who have fallen, only to fall into the same temptations themselves. Be humble or you will stumble.

Temperance

We must also practice our weapon of temperance. Temperance is an inner strength that comes from the Holy Spirit. "LORD, I cry unto thee: make haste unto me; give ear unto my voice, when I cry unto thee. Let my prayer be set forth before thee as incense; and the lifting up of my hands as the evening sacrifice. Set a watch, O LORD, before my mouth; keep the door of my lips" (Psalm 141:1-3, KJV). Success in God's kingdom is P.O.L.I.T.I.C.A.L. (Power Of Life Is in the Tongue; It Creates & Affirms Life). Master the arsenal of the fruit of the Spirit and use it daily.

Acronym to Remember: **P.O.L.I.T.I.C.A.L.**
(**P**ower **O**f **L**ife **I**s in the **T**ongue; **I**t **C**reates & **A**ffirms **L**ife)

Verse to Remember:
"Moderation is better than muscle, self-control better than political power" (Proverbs 16:32, The Message).

Questions of the Day:
• What are the politics of God's kingdom?

• What are some weapons Satan uses to fight against us?

- What are the works of the flesh? (See Galatians 5:19-22.)

- What weapons do we, as Christians, have in our arsenal to combat evil?

- Name the nine fruits of the Spirit.

- How would you rate your proficiency in the use of the nine spiritual weapons?

- How do you plan to become more proficient?

DAY 32

Must
Only
Use
To
Heal

Death and life are in the power of the tongue: and they that loveth it shall eat the fruit thereof.

—Proverbs 18:21, KJV

Proverbs says, "A good man shall be satisfied with the fruit of his mouth; but the souls of the wicked shall perish" (Proverbs 13:2, Ancient Eastern Text). The question we have to ask ourselves is, "What am I confessing?"

Christianity is called "the Great Confession." "To confess" means "to declare, decide, or decree." What are you decreeing?

You will also decree a thing, and it will be established for you;
And light will shine on your ways.

—Job 22:28, NASB

Years ago, I used to think I was dumb. The negative confession began as a child. My first-grade teacher used me as an example for one of my classmates who was having difficulty with reading. She said, "Eddie's reading at level three, and he's black. Are you going to let a black child pass you by?" I internalized her negative belief about black people and failed first grade.

You must be careful what you say to yourself and others, especially children. God will judge you accordingly. "Truly I tell you, just as you did it to one of the least of these who are members of my family, you did it to me" (Matthew 25:40, NRSV).

Words kill, words give life;
they're either poison or fruit—you choose.

—Proverbs 18:21, The Message

"For by your words you will be justified, and by your words you will be condemned" (Matthew 12:37, NASB).

Many people do not comprehend the power of their mouths. Jesus admonished some of his disciples, "Then do you also fail to understand? Do you not see that whatever goes into a person from outside cannot defile ... It is what comes out of a person that defiles" (Mark 7:18-20, NRSV).

When Jesus healed the blind man and said, "According to your faith be it unto you" (Matthew 9:29, KJV), he was essentially saying, "According to the condition of your H.E.A.R.T. (Higher Empowerment Abides Resourcefully Therein) ..." "For out of the abundance of the heart the mouth speaks" (Matthew 12:34, NKJV).

The negative thinking and prejudices that are inside your heart flow out of your mouth naturally. If you believe in your heart that you are poor, you will confess that you are poor. If you believe in your heart that you are rich, you will confess wealth. If you believe in your heart that you are sick, you will confess sickness. If you believe in your heart "that by his stripes I am healed" (Isaiah 53:5, personal translation), you will confess health. If you believe in your heart that one nationality is superior or inferior to yours, then you will confess it with your mouth.

We are all equal in the eyes of God. "Peter opened his mouth, and said, Of a truth I perceive that God is no respecter of persons: but in every nation he that feareth him, and worketh righteousness, is accepted with him" (Acts 10:34-35, KJV). "Every nation" includes every nationality of individuals that respects God and works in righteousness. The word *righteousness,* in its original Greek equivalent *dikaiosune,*[1] means "equity of character."

The Lord continues to reveal to me that the dis-ease in the confession of our mouths originates in our hearts. Therefore, we must be transformed by the renewing of our minds; I believe this can be done through prayer or through regular practice of H.E.A.R.T. Meditation™.

As you are transforming your mind,
  Above all else, guard your heart,
    for it is the wellspring of life.

---

1. *James Strong,* The Exhaustive Concordance of the Bible *(Nashville, Abingdon, 1890),* "Greek Dictionary of the New Testament," *#1343.*

Put away perversity from your mouth;
   keep corrupt talk far from your lips.
                                    —Proverbs 4:23-24, NIV
   Don't speak death upon yourself or others through negative confession. Speak life—M.O.U.T.H. (Must Only Use To Heal).

Acronym to Remember: **M.O.U.T.H.**
(**M**ust **O**nly **U**se **T**o **H**eal)

Verse to Remember:
"Death and life are in the power of the tongue: and they that love it shall eat the fruit thereof" (Proverbs 18:21, KJV).

Questions of the Day:
• What has Christianity been called?

• Define *confession*.

• How have you personally been affected by negative confessions of others?

- How have you personally been affected by positive confessions of others?

- To whom have you spoken a negative confession?

- What are your plans to mitigate any potential damage?

DAY 33

G ift
O f
S tupidity
S tagnating
I ts
P ractitioners

Though some tongues just love the taste of gossip, Christians have better use for language than that. Don't talk dirty or silly. That kind of talk doesn't fit our style.

—Ephesians 5:3, The Message

A while back I watched *Larry King Live* on television, as I sometimes do. His guest that evening was businessman and original Jackson Five member Jermaine Jackson. A viewer called into the show and said, "Can you tell me if your brother Michael is heterosexual, bisexual, asexual, or transsexual?"

Jermaine handled the question graciously and with much class. He said something to the effect of "All I know is my brother Michael is a wonderful person. You would have to ask him about his sex life."

The question about Michael Jackson's sexual preference, as well as that of other celebrities, has been posed for years in barbershops, beauty salons, and other social settings. Based on those speculations, many false rumors about people we don't even know have been spread. As a result, innocent people get hurt. We have to be careful not to participate in gossip.

> Listening to gossip is like eating cheap candy;
> do you really want junk like that in your belly?
>
> —Proverbs 18:8, The Message

We can all probably relate incidents from our own lives when we were hurt by gossip. Friendships are particularly damaged by this practice.

Churches can be destroyed by gossip. Loyalties erode, energy lags, and the focus shifts from Christ to individual personalities.

Solomon said,

> The words of a fool start fights;
>> do him a favor and gag him.
>
> —Proverbs 18:6, The Message

Solomon's father, David, had the right idea about gossips. In a psalm he wrote on behalf of God,

> I put a gag on the gossip
>> who bad-mouths his neighbor;
> I can't stand
>> arrogance.
> But I have my eyes on the salt-of-the-earth people;
>> they're the ones I want working with me;
> Men and women on the straight and narrow—
>> these are the ones I want at my side.
> But no one who traffics in lies
>> gets a job with me; I have no patience with liars.
> I've rounded up all the wicked like cattle
>> and herded them right out of the country.
>
> —Psalm 101:5-8, The Message

God does the same things with gossips.

False accusations not only hurt other people but also can keep you out of the presence of God. David asked,

> LORD, who may dwell in your sanctuary?
>> Who may live on your holy hill?
>
> —Psalm 15:1, NIV

The answer is this:

> He whose walk is blameless
>> and who does what is righteous,
> who speaks the truth from his heart
>> and has no slander on his tongue,
> who does his neighbor no wrong
>> and casts no slur on his fellowman.
>
> —Psalm 15:2-3, NIV

If you want to be successful in God's kingdom, and operate in the kingdom in which we live with God's and people's favor, there are four things you should do:

1. Dwell in the presence of God.

2. Stay out of other people's bedrooms, with the exception of the one you share with your spouse.

3. When you find a gossip in your midst, follow the Word of God: "Warn a divisive person once, and then warn him a second time. After that, have nothing to do with him" (Titus 3:10, NIV).

4. Do not allow yourself to get baited into gossip.

When someone tries to bait you into providing an answer about someone or something you don't know, be careful how you respond. I can tell you from experience that your words can get stretched out of proportion and give strength to rumors.

Years ago, someone asked me if a colleague of ours was gay. I told that person that I didn't know; our colleague didn't discuss his sex life with me and it was none of my business. I should have ended my response there, but I didn't. I added, "I have wondered about that. I never hear him discussing an interest in women." I spoke too much. My last two sentences were taken out of context and were spread as a rumor. As a result, I became a troublemaker. "Troublemakers listen to troublemakers" (Proverbs 17:4, CEV). I had some serious repenting to do.

Don't even listen to gossip or read gossip columns or magazines. When someone tries to draw you into unbecoming discourse, respond with dignity and class, and don't get drawn in. "Let your conversation be always full of grace, seasoned with salt, so that you may know how to answer everyone" (Colossians 4:6, NIV).

Jesus was a master at avoiding traps. The Sadducees and Pharisees were always trying to get him caught up in "he-said/she-said" messes in hopes of destroying him.

> Keeping a close watch on him, they sent spies, who pretended to be honest. They hoped to catch Jesus in something he said so that they might hand him over to the power and authority of the governor. So the spies questioned him: "Teacher, we know that you speak and teach what is right, and that you do not show partiality but teach the

way of God in accordance with the truth. Is it right for us to pay taxes to Caesar or not?"

He saw through their duplicity and said to them, "Show me a denarius. Whose portrait and inscription are on it?"

"Caesar's," they replied.

He said to them, "Then give to Caesar what is Caesar's, and to God what is God's."

They were unable to trap him in what he had said there in public. And astonished by his answer, they became silent.

—Luke 20:20-26, NIV

Jesus applied a method that salespeople call "handling objections." He handled his opponents' hidden objections according to discernment. He listened and acknowledged that he was listening. He explored their question by presenting them with a question, then responded according to their answer. This shut them up.

The devil is called the "accuser of our brethren" (Revelation 12:10, KJV). Gossip is a deadly trap of the devil; we must follow Jesus' example to avoid it.

"Be ye therefore wise as serpents, and harmless as doves" (Matthew 10:16, KJV). God is calling you to a higher standard of being and doing. To maintain your rank, and to advance to higher levels on earth and in the kingdom of God, wisdom is required. As Jesus said, "I tell you that men will have to give account on the day of judgment for every careless word they have spoken. For by your words you will be acquitted, and by your words you will be condemned" (Matthew 12:36-37, NIV).

Don't get caught up in G.O.S.S.I.P. (Gift Of Stupidity Stagnating Its Practitioners).

Acronym to Remember: **G.O.S.S.I.P.**
(Gift Of Stupidity Stagnating Its Practitioners)

Verse to Remember:
"Though some tongues just love the taste of gossip, Christians have better use for language than that. Don't talk dirty or silly. That kind of talk doesn't fit our style" (Ephesians 5:3, The Message).

Questions of the Day:
- According to Psalm 15, who may dwell in God's sanctuary?

- Describe a time when you have been hurt by gossip.

- According to Titus 3:10, how should you handle a gossip?

- What will you do the next time someone tries to involve you in gossip?

- If strife has been created as a result of gossip, how can we put it out? (Read Proverbs 26:20 and Matthew 18:15-17.)

DAY 34

T raditional
E ntrapment/Ecclesiastical
A partheid
R estricts
S pirit

See to it that no one takes you captive through hollow and deceptive philosophy, which depends on human tradition and the basic principles of this world rather than on Christ.

–Colossians 2:8, NIV

Don't let yourselves get taken in by religious smooth talk. God gets furious with people who are full of religious sales talk but want nothing to do with him.

–Ephesians 5:6-7, The Message

Doing things the way they have always been done for no other reason than "That's the way we've always done it" is traditional entrapment. The word *ecclesiastical* refers to the organization of the church. Apartheid is discrimination.

Jesus broke tradition, challenging people to think outside the box of religion and to be doers of the Word and not just hearers. Because of this, he experienced discrimination. There were many places where his message was not welcomed. Some religious people even wanted to kill him.

The traditional entrapment of the religious mindset in ministry has circumvented the destinies of many people who have been called and ordained by God. God calls them to do great things, some of which may never have been done before. Not submitting to God's will, they respond, "I have to go and get permission from my pastor first, because I am submitted under his authority." Thank God that Jesus was not under religious bondage. Had he submitted to the authority of some religious leaders, we would all be in big trouble today.

An older gentleman shared his testimony. He worked as a janitor in the church. In his youth he felt a call upon his life. He met with his pastor and told him that he believed God was calling him to the ministry. The pastor told him to keep coming to prayer meetings and continue working in the church. For many years he taught Sunday school and waited for his pastor to respond to his call. The tradition of the church required that the pastor license him before he could operate as a minister, which he believed was his calling.

He waited for the pastor to take his hand and lead him into the ministry. He served in the church for many years and the pastor never licensed him. Years later, his pastor died. The man felt he never walked in his calling. As he looked back over his life, he believes he should have just gone to seminary as he felt the Holy Spirit was leading him to do. By waiting on the approval of another, he missed a calling. There is no telling where God would have led him had he aggressively answered that call. Instead, he put his trust in a human being.

This is what the LORD says:

"Cursed is the one who trusts in man,
    who depends on flesh for his strength
    and whose heart turns away from the Lord.
He will be like a bush in wastelands;
    he will not see prosperity when it comes.
He will dwell in the parched places of the desert."

—Jeremiah 17:5-6, NIV

"Flesh" refers to people's own understanding. There are serious consequences to trusting in human beings instead of God. You curse yourself.

I agree that when you are thinking of doing something within the church, or if you are using the name of the church, you require permission from the overseer. It is also wise to inform him or her of what you are being led to do if it might create conflict. However, when God tells you to do something, don't seek someone else's permission. You have *God's* permission. Be led by the Spirit. "Many are called, but few are chosen" (Matthew 22:14, KJV). God calls many, but few of us choose to answer.

God wants us to do what God told us to do without adding layers of complexity that hinder the flow of Spirit. In business, ministry, and civic groups, people have submitted their divine ideas to people with whom God did not tell them to share them. They were told by them, "Great idea. Let's set up a committee and execute your idea." The idea was executed all right. It died in committee. It is important that we do what God tells us, nothing more and nothing less. Did God tell you to share your vision with your pastor?

I have heard pastors ask people to put their visions on hold and assist them with theirs. Delaying your response to God's call this way may be unwise. It can anger God when we don't respond to a divine call. If you don't do what God tells you to do—when God tells you to do it—you won't be where you need to be to receive what God wants to give to you. Timing is important. If you were running a relay race and your teammate handed you the baton, and if you delayed executing your portion of the run, the whole team could be affected.

This is what the LORD says:

> "Where is your mother's certificate of divorce
>   with which I sent her away?
> Or to which of my creditors
>   did I sell you?
> Because of your sins you were sold;
>   because of your transgressions your mother was sent away.
> When I came, why was there no one?
>   When I called, why was there no one to answer?"
>
> —Isaiah 50:1-2, NIV

If God is still God, then we must obey. Have you put someone else in God's place? You are not a slave to anyone. "If the Son sets you free, you will be free indeed" (John 8:36, NIV). You are free to do what you were born to do. If you have placed yourself in bondage, that was your choice. It was not God's doing.

"To sin" means "to fall short of the mark." By delaying, you may not be in place when Jesus returns. He called you, and you didn't answer. Are you still delaying running your leg of the race? "Teach us to number our days, that we may apply our hearts unto wisdom" (Psalm 90:12, KJV). Your days are numbered; you may not have time to delay any longer.

When the Spirit is leading you, you might procrastinate in following. In your mind, it may not make any sense to even go there. Had Jesus been submitted under traditional entrapment, I doubt if they would have permitted him to go into a bad neighborhood, where there were people who were Satan worshipers, prostitutes, drug dealers, and murderers. The leaders would have feared that it could hurt their image.

I once heard a pastor tell some volunteer ministers, "If you have any speaking engagements, you must discuss them with me. Some places that may invite you to speak, God is not there." He went on to say, "I want to make sure that where you speak is acceptable, and I'd like to go over your speech with you to make certain that you are saying what saith the Lord." My spirit said, "Run—don't walk—to the nearest exit! A lid, not a covering, is about to be placed over you." If God is not present at a certain place, God will be when I show up, because I'm taking Jesus, whom I represent, with me.

Jesus, being led by the Spirit, went down into hell, where he preached a revival and set people free.

"When he ascended on high he made
    captivity itself a captive;
    he gave gifts to his people."

—Ephesians 4:8, NRSV

Going where God leads you may conflict with tradition. "Jesus said, 'It is not the healthy who need a doctor, but the sick' " (Matthew 9:12, NIV). Wherever people are hurting, we need to take off our blinders and allow God to lead us there, so that God uses us to heal them, as he did his Son, Jesus. Many of us are afraid to be led by the Spirit because we have bought the idea that we need the authority of another. Some people are convinced that if they don't have the blessing of their temporal rather than spiritual "high priest" (their temporal high priest being the human being under whom they have submitted themselves), God's anointing won't be upon them. People who think like this have submitted themselves to a spirit of bondage called fear that is not of God. Instead of receiving a covering, a lid has been placed over them.

"God hath not given us the spirit of fear; but of power, and of love, and of a sound mind" (2 Timothy 1:7, KJV). Foolishly, we allow people to anoint us with the spirit of fear so they can try to manipulate and control the spirit that God has placed within us. God will not permit the Spirit to be used like that. In this awareness, we are to boldly go and do what God tells us to do. A greater anointing than any mere mortal could give is upon all who obey God and walk in their calling.

If some want to help with your expenses and cover you, great! If they don't, you already have a covering—that of God. When God's call is upon your life, God is the only one who can fully cover you. Those whom you may look to for support may not support you or understand what God is doing in your life. Don't be disappointed. God gave you the vision. God chose you. If you are expecting others to understand, you may be in for a rude awakening. Being led by the Spirit will save you from crying T.E.A.R.S. (Traditional Entrapment/Ecclesiastical Apartheid Restricting Spirit).

Many people may make promises to you, such as "If you just put your ministry on hold and assist me with mine, I'll take care of you."

Thus says the LORD:

"Cursed is the man who trusts in man
And makes flesh his strength."

—Jeremiah 17:5, NKJV

We can use the past for instruction and our future for construction. The Israelites of old put their trust in people, and look at what happened.

Bitterly she weeps at night,
tears are upon her cheeks.
Among all her lovers
there is none to comfort her...;
they have become her enemies.

—Lamentations 1:2, NIV

"She was not mindful of her end; therefore her glory is low; she has no comforter" (Lamentations 1:9, Ancient Eastern Text).

Jesus was mindful of his end. He said, "My meat is to do the will of him that sent me, and to finish his work" (John 4:34, KJV). He didn't seek permission from religious leaders to heal the sick or cast out demons.

People can arrest the call that's upon your life if you let them. "Do not grieve the Holy Spirit of God, with whom you were sealed for the day of redemption" (Ephesians 4:30, NIV). God won't use you if you don't allow

God to do so. Granting other people permission to put a lid over you produces T.E.A.R.S. (Traditional Entrapment/Ecclesiastical Apartheid
Restricting Spirit).

Acronym to Remember: **T.E.A.R.S.**
(**T**raditional **E**ntrapment/**E**cclesiastical **A**partheid
Restricting **S**pirit)

Verse to Remember:
"See to it that no one takes you captive through hollow and deceptive
philosophy, which depends on human tradition and the basic principles
of this world rather than on Christ" (Colossians 2:8, NIV).

Questions of the Day:
• What is traditional entrapment?

• How did Jesus break tradition?

• List some things that God, through your prayer and meditation, has
  been calling you to do.

- Read Jeremiah 17:5. What can happen when a person puts his or her trust in another person instead of following the voice of God?

- What are some things God has called you to do that you have put off doing?

- What has stopped you?

DAY 35

T he
R oot
E mpowers
E verything

If the primary root of the tree is holy, there's bound to be some holy fruit.

—Romans 11:16, The Message

Each year, many of us go out and buy live Christmas trees. The tree, having been cut at the root, will be placed in a stand in our homes. We'll fill the stand with water in an effort to keep the tree alive a little longer. After the holidays, if we planted the tree in the backyard, it would not grow. In spite of the fact that the tree is still green and beautiful, it would continue dying, because it has no root.

That's what happens when motivation is without divine inspiration. It sounds and feels good for a short season, but it cannot grow because it has no root. The Word of God is the root of inspiration.

"Blessed (happy, fortunate, prosperous and enviable) is the man who walks and lives not in the counsel of the ungodly [following their advice, their plans and purposes], nor stands [submissive and inactive] in the path where sinners walk, nor sits down [to relax and rest] where the scornful [and the mockers] gather. But his delight and desire are in the law of the Lord, and on His law (the precepts, and instructions, the teachings of God) he habitually meditates (ponders and studies) by day and by night [Romans 13:8-10; Galatians 3:1-29; II Timothy 3:16]. And he shall be like a tree firmly planted [and tended] by the streams of water, ready to bring forth its fruit in its season; its leaf also shall not fade or wither; and everything he does shall prosper [and come to maturity] [Jeremiah 17:7,8]."

—Psalm 1:1-2, Amplified Bible, Old Testament

Those of us who truly want to succeed in our spiritual walk must ask ourselves, *Am I interested in essence or nescience?* Webster defines essence as "the inward nature of anything, underlying its manifestations." The inner being is what God is most concerned with (Psalm 51:6). Webster defines *nescience* as "lacking knowledge; ignorant." Webster's second definition of the word *nescience* is *agnostic,* "a person who believes that the human mind cannot know whether there is a God or an ultimate cause, or anything beyond material phenomena."

The true manifestation of spiritual growth is in the Word. "In the beginning was the Word, and the Word was with God, and the Word was God" (John 1:1, KJV).

"Therefore, my dear friends, as you have always obeyed—not only in my presence, but now much more in my absence—continue to work out your salvation with fear and trembling, for it is God who works in you to will and to act according to his good purpose" (Philippians 2:12-13, NIV). "Fear," in this instance, does not mean "to be afraid." It means "to revere or respect." Just as a person who knows how to swim is not afraid of the ocean, but rather has a respect for its power, so are we to respect the Word of God and use it to navigate the waters of life.

Start reading and hearing God's Word. There are 1,089 chapters in the Bible. If you read just three chapters a day, you can read the whole Bible in one year. Read one to two chapters of the Bible in the morning and another one to two chapters at night, firmly planting your tree by the streams of water.

I find it beneficial to listen to the Bible as well as reading it daily. I ride the treadmill or get on the Stairmaster almost daily. During my exercise, I listen to the tape series *James Earl Jones Reads the Bible.* "Faith comes from hearing, and hearing by the word of Christ" (Romans 10:17, NASB). As you get the Word of God in you, you are cultivating the root of your soul. If you are obeying the Word, whatever God has for you will spring forth like a T.R.E.E. in due season.

Acronym to Remember: **T.R.E.E.**
(**T**he **R**oot **E**mpowers **E**verything)

Verse to Remember:
"If the primary root of the tree is holy, there's bound to be some holy fruit" (Romans 11:16, The Message).

Questions of the Day:
• If the root of your tree is holy, what can you expect?

• What can you do to make the primary root of your tree holy?

• If you are not already doing so, when will you begin reading several Bible chapters a day?

• What did you learn from today's reading, and with whom can you share it?

Overcoming obstacles

DAY 36

D on't
E mbrace
S in;
I t
R etards
E verything

In righteousness shall you be established; you shall be far from oppression, you shall not fear; and from ruin, for destruction shall not come near you.

—Isaiah 54:14, Ancient Eastern Text

His own iniquities will capture the wicked,
And he will be held with the cords of his sin.

—Proverbs 5:22, NASB

While moving furniture, I received a powerful revelation. You and I are connected to everything we desire.

One of the most complicated items to move was my entertainment system, with its overkill of cables and cords. To make it easier to reinstall the sound component of the system, I decided to leave the speaker stands intact and the speaker connections plugged into the amplifier.

One of my friends and I laid a large moving blanket on the floor, placed the intact components on the blanket, and carried the system out to the truck. It was so awkward carrying the system in this manner, and our methodology actually made the reinstalling more complicated. During the move, these long wires became tangled. I had to trace and untangle each wire in order to pull each speaker from the amplifier and place it back into its proper place.

Our connection to our desires is much the same way. The word *desire,* in its Latin root word, means "from the Father." God has already connected you to your desires. There is a cord connecting you to the mate whom God has chosen for you, the home, the career, or the lifestyle of your dreams. The evidence of this connection is in your faith. "Now faith is the substance of things hoped for, the evidence of things not seen" (Hebrews 11:1, KJV).

You and I are irresistible magnets that attract all things that belong to us by divine right. The strength to draw godly desires is in your faith. "According to your faith be it unto you" (Matthew 9:29, KJV). One of the reasons some of us have difficulty pulling what we desire is that our faith is weak. Nevertheless, some of us with strong faith are pulling what we desire, but it just isn't coming to us. We remind God of Mark 11:24. "Lord, you said in your Word that, whatsoever I desire, when I pray and believe that I have received it, I shall have it." We just don't understand why the things we are asking for are not coming to us. A possible reason these things are not coming to you could be that your wires are tangled. "When you ask, you do not receive, because you ask with wrong motives, that you may spend what you get on your pleasures" (James 4:3, NIV).

Husbands, if God blessed you with the woman of your dreams, what are you going to do with that person? How are you going to treat her? Do you have any issues in your life that would cause you not to obey Ephesians 5:25-26: "Husbands, love your wives, just as Christ loved the church and gave himself up for her to make her holy, cleansing her by the washing with water through the word"? Christ gave the church identity, security, and stability. He is described as "the Rock" (1 Corinthians 10:4). These same provisions are what we as men are to provide for our wives and children. For many women, a sense of security is tied closely to her relationship with her husband. If your love of career, football, or outings with your friends lead to negligence in your marriage, your wires are tangled. As you adapt to the ways of Christ, you likely will become more sensitive to the needs and wants of the person to whom you are committed in love.

"Wives, be subject—be submissive and adapt yourselves—to your own husbands as [a service] to the Lord" (Ephesians 5:22, The Amplified New Testament). To submit does not mean to forego your education, skill, or God-given strengths and talents, but to adapt yourself to your husband, just as it would be wise for him to adapt to your innate strengths and acquired skills. For example, if your husband's strength is in finance, respect his abilities and encourage him to develop his gifts in this area. If we are not careful, jealousy and competition can enter into the marriage relationship, sometimes so subtly that we don't realize it. That's why trust is so important. Trust not only with regard to motives, but also in the area of giftedness. Respect your mate and the gifts and talents God has given him. Even if you do not always understand or agree, as long as you know that he is a man of integrity, your trust is well-placed.

When God blesses you with the wealth you are seeking, what are you going to do with it? Are you going to tithe at least a tenth of it? Are you going to "contribute to the needs of God's people [sharing in the necessities of the saints]; pursue the practice of hospitality" (Romans 12:13, The Amplified New Testament)? Will you try to make others envious of your success, especially those you feel have wronged you? "Bless those who persecute you [who are cruel in their attitude toward you]; bless and do not curse them" (Romans 12:14, The Amplified New Testament).

If you are unwilling to submit to God's ways, the wires connecting you to your desires are tangled, and that will make it almost impossible to pull your desires. "But thou shalt remember the LORD thy God: for it is [God] that giveth thee power to get wealth" (Deuteronomy 8:18, KJV).

Your power to gain wealth, your magnetic field, will increase by untangling the cords in your life. You will be able to do as it is written: "God … calleth those things which be not as though they were" (Romans 4:17, KJV).

Identifying all your desires and then identifying those that conflict with God's ways accomplishes the untangling. Make a list of all of your desires and see if you have any conflicts. For example, God desires that we "seek … first the kingdom of God, and his righteousness; and all these things shall be added unto you" (Matthew 6:33, KJV). You may even have this listed as a desire. But you might also have a desire to engage in ungodly behavior. Your desire to sin conflicts with your desire to seek the kingdom of God and all of its righteousness. As a result of this conflict, everything else, including your dreams and desires, can't be pulled to you, because your wires are tangled.

Untangle your wires by doing as Jesus did when he said to God, "Not my will, but thine, be done" (Luke 22:42, KJV). Give into God's ways and allow God to lead you to your destiny. Do you trust God?

Acronym to Remember: **D.E.S.I.R.E.**
(**D**on't **E**mbrace **S**in; **I**t **R**etards **E**verything)

Verse to Remember:
"Delight thyself also in the LORD; and he shall give thee the desires of thine heart. Commit thy way unto the LORD; trust also in him; and he shall bring it to pass" (Psalm 37:4-5, KJV).

Questions of the Day:
• What are some specific things that you desire? (Make a thorough, uninhibited list.)

• When God blesses you with those desires, what are you going to do with them?

• How willing are you to submit completely to God's ways? This includes tithing and abstaining from sexual sin.

- What cords do you have tangled?

- What did you learn from today's reading, and with whom can you share it?

DAY 37

L and mines
O f
T he
S oul

You shall know the truth, and the truth shall make you free.

—John 8:32, NKJV

What is a "lot"? The Hebrew word for *lot* means "veil or covering."[1] It symbolizes a dangerous part of us that is subconsciously hidden like a land mine.

A land mine is an explosive device designed to maim or kill the person who triggers it. Because land mines are hidden under the surface of the ground, people do not realize they have triggered one until after they have stepped on it. Mines are indiscriminate in terms of target and time. They go on killing and maiming soldiers and civilians, men and women, adults and children alike decades after the fighting has ended. To keep innocent people from dying, much focus in recent years has been put on removing the land mines.

Many of us have land mines hidden deep in our souls. Land mines of the soul were uncovered in Denzel Washington's movie *Antwone Fisher*, which is based on a true story. Fisher was a decent, young Navy soldier. However, he often got into fights. His temper was easily set off. His commander sent him to a psychiatrist, played by Washington, for evaluation. Initially, Fisher didn't realize he had any problems and didn't want to talk. The psychiatrist got him to open up. Fisher was then able to see that he had L.O.T.S. (Land mines Of The Soul). Antwone revealed that he had been repeatedly molested and physically and emotionally abused by his caregivers while in foster care.

---

1. *James Strong,* The Exhaustive Concordance of the Bible *(Madison, N.J.: Published by James Strong, 1890), "Hebrew and Chaldee Dictionary," #3875.*

Prior to the release of the movie in 2002, Barbara Walters did a *20/20* interview with Fisher, Washington, and the young man who played Fisher in the movie. She asked Antwone, "How come you didn't report it?"

Antwone told her, "I was afraid."

Millions of children each year are the victims of sexual abuse. The perpetrator is often a family member, family friend, or neighbor. In such cases, children hesitate to report abuse because of the fear that disclosure will bring consequences even worse than being victimized again. The victim may fear consequences from the family, feel guilty for consequences to the perpetrator, and may fear subsequent retaliatory actions from the perpetrator.

The devil's purpose is to kill, maim, and destroy. Even though he has already been defeated, he is killing, maiming, and destroying lives and families. Things have happened in many of our lives that are embarrassing or hurtful. Instead of dealing with them, we bury the pain deep in our souls. The pain becomes a land mine; if someone steps on it, we explode, injuring ourselves as well as innocent victims.

What are the land mines of your soul? Even the most together people have some deep issues that they have buried deep in the ground of their souls to keep from dealing with them. As Antwone dug up his land mines, he inspired his psychiatrist to do the same. The psychiatrist and his wife had hidden marital problems that stemmed from the fact that they were unable to have children. The doctor sought help for his wife. However, he did not think he had a problem. Nevertheless, he was emotionally disconnected from his wife. He dug up his land mines and saved his marriage.

As I mentioned earlier, one of the issues I had was the way I was born— as the result of an affair. The pain from this was buried deep inside me. For a long time, I had trust issues. The thing that I feared came to pass. My wife also had an affair and conceived a child. If the land mines of our souls are not removed, we can attract the very things that we fear (Job 3:25).

What issues do you have in your life that you have not confronted? What effects, if any, have these issues had in your life?

A young lady was promiscuous. When asked why this was so, she said she didn't know. However, she was wise enough to see that she had a problem. She sought the help of a pastoral counselor and found her land mine. A male family member had molested her as a child. She had buried this horrible memory deep inside. After she delved more deeply, she saw that this was a pattern that ran in her family. Her mother had been molested repeatedly by a family member as a child, and so had all of her aunts and sister. Uncovering her land mine probably saved her life and helped to break the cycle.

The devil wants you to keep your personal and family secrets buried deep in the underground so that they can continue to influence you. There, once triggered, they can turn into explosive situations. He can get two for one, destroy a whole family, or, sometimes, whole churches or communities. All someone has to do is to trigger your land mine. Deeper issues that were ignored often trigger promiscuity, violent rages, depression, suicide, and physical sickness.

If something is bothering you, don't hold it in. Dig it up. Talk to God, and to a person whom you trust and who can help you too, such as a parent, a pastor, a counselor, or a wise friend.

Acronym to Remember: **L.O.T.S.**
(**L**and mines **O**f **T**he **S**oul)

Verse to Remember:
"You shall know the truth, and the truth shall make you free" (John 8:32, NKJV).

Questions of the Day:
• What are the land mines of your soul?

- What issues do you have in your life that you have not confronted?

- What effects have these issues had in your life?

- What did you learn from today's reading, and with whom can you share it?

DAY 38

Trouble
Experienced
Steadfastly
Trusting

Don't be bewildered or surprised when you go through the fiery trials ahead, for this is no strange, unusual thing that is going to happen to you.

—1 Peter 4:12, TLB

It is the fire of suffering that brings about the gold of godliness.

—Madame Guyon

Has there ever been a time in your life when it seemed like Murphy's Law was taking over, when whatever could go wrong seemed to go wrong? Some of us experience difficulty and just give up. Some experience difficulty and give in to the temptation to sin.

The lost-and-found of dreams is filled with the dreams of those who just gave up. The prisons are full of people who gave in to temptation. Money became lean, and they gave in to the urge to sell drugs, commit robbery, or commit some other crime.

While I was speaking at a prison recently, a seemingly intelligent man was in the audience. After my presentation, I asked him, "What landed you in prison?" He said the enemy was working against him. He lost his job, started selling drugs to provide for him and his family, and got caught.

When circumstances seem to work against us, many of us are quick to say, "It's the enemy working against me." Sometimes we are correct. However, we make our own choices and are responsible for them. The devil can be like weights used to help you work out your salvation. Think about it—if you went to the gym regularly and worked out only with light weights, your muscles would not grow. There wouldn't be enough resistance placed on them to force growth. Progressive resistance is required to grow physically, mentally, and spiritually. Because of this, Paul advised, "Work out (cultivate, carry out the goal, and fully complete) your own salvation" (Philippians 2:12, The Amplified New Testament).

The devil continues to exist only because God allows him to exist. We can actually grow through the trials and temptations of the deceiver.

"One day when the angels came to report to GOD, Satan, who was the Designated Accuser, came along with them" (Job 1:6, The Message). Satan would not be allowed to come before the Lord unless he also had to report to God.

GOD singled out Satan and said, "What have you been up to?"
Satan answered GOD, "Going here and there, checking things out on earth."

—Job 1:7, The Message

Satan obviously could not find anyone who was a worthy challenge for him. The people he had scoured the earth and found were like some Christians: they had one foot in the church and the other foot on a banana peel. It was too easy to cause them to slip and fall into temptation. It was not worth his time to even bother with them.

"Then the LORD said to Satan, 'Have you considered my servant Job? There is no one on earth like him; he is blameless and upright, a man who fears God and shuns evil'" (Job 1:8, NIV). Why would God call Satan's attention to one of God's loyal servants? God knew Job would pass the test and mature even more through the test.

Job had spent a lot of time with God. When you spend time with God, God teaches you and imparts wisdom. When you were in school, what did your teachers do after they had taught you? They tested you to confirm that you had indeed mastered the lesson. If you passed the exam, you were allowed to progress to the next challenging level. If you failed, you had to repeat the same lesson.

Satan was still not convinced that Job was a good challenge. "Satan retorted, 'So do you think Job does all that out of sheer goodness of his heart? Why, no one ever had it so good! You pamper him like a pet, make sure that nothing bad ever happens to him or his family or his possessions, bless everything he does—he can't lose!'" (Job 1:9-10, The Message).

Satan said to God,

"But what do you think would happen if you reached down and took away everything that is his? He'd curse you right to your face, that's what."

God replied, "We'll see. Go ahead—do what you want with all that is his. Just don't hurt him."

—Job 1:11-12, The Message

God gave Satan permission to destroy Job's family and take his wealth and health. "His wife said to him, 'Are you still holding on to your integrity? Curse God and die!'" (Job 2:9, NIV). Throughout the whole ordeal, Job remained faithful to God and passed his T.E.S.T.S. (Trouble Experienced Steadfastly Trusting Spirit).

Job's friends began to talk badly about him when calamity came upon him and his household. They questioned his righteousness and even turned against him. His friend Elihu even claimed to speak for God when he spoke against Job. Job prayed for them.

"After Job had interceded for his friends, GOD restored his fortune—and then doubled it!… The LORD blessed the latter part of Job's life more than the first" (Job 42:10, 12, NIV). Job was blessed with more wealth, more children, and a long life.

To pass life's tests, you must do four things:

1. Be led by the Spirit.
2. Know the Word of God.
3. Speak the Word to your situation.
4. Act upon the Word.

Before Jesus was allowed to complete his assignment on earth by dying on Calvary for us, he was led by the Spirit into the wilderness to be tempted by the devil. The devil came to him at his weakest moment, after he had fasted forty days and forty nights.

"The tempter came to Jesus and said, 'If you are the Son of God, tell these stones to become bread'" (Matthew 4:3, NIV). Jesus knew the Word of God. Therefore, he knew how to respond. "Jesus answered, by quoting Deuteronomy: It takes more than bread to stay alive. It takes a steady stream of words from God's mouth" (Matthew 4:4, The Message).

The devil does not stop with one test. He came at Jesus in a different way. For the second test the Devil took him to the Holy City. He sat him on top of the Temple and said, "Since you are God's Son, jump." The Devil goaded him by quoting Psalm 91: "He has placed you in the care of angels. They will catch you so that you won't so much as stub your toe on a stone."

Jesus countered with another citation from Deuteronomy: "Don't you dare test the Lord your God."

For the third test, the Devil took him on the peak of a huge mountain. He gestured expansively, pointing out all the earth's kingdoms, how glorious they all were. Then he said, "They're yours—lock, stock, and barrel. Just go down on your knees and worship me, and they're yours."

Jesus' refusal was curt: "Beat it, Satan!" He backed his rebuke with a third quotation from Deuteronomy: "Worship the Lord your God, and only him. Serve him with absolute single-heartedness."

The Test was over. The Devil left. And in his place, angels! Angels came and took care of Jesus' needs.

—Matthew 4:5-11, The Message

Had Jesus failed his tests, he would not have been allowed to die on Calvary, and all of us would have suffered. Jesus gave up everything so that you and I could have everything.

When I am challenged with T.E.S.T.S. (Trouble Experienced Steadfastly Trusting Spirit), I remind myself that a great many people are counting on me to make the right decision and pull through this. The one whom God has ordained for me to marry is counting on me. Our children who are yet to be born are counting on me. The people whose lives will be touched by the work God is using me for are counting on me. More importantly, God is counting on me, just as God was counting on Job and Jesus to pass their tests.

God is also counting on you. Be led by the Spirit. Study and learn the Word of God. Speak the Word to every situation by which you are challenged, and act upon the Word. Although God may allow you to be tried in the fire, you are being burnished G.O.L.D. (God-Ordained Life Development).

Acronym to Remember: **T.E.S.T.**
(**T**rouble **E**xperienced **S**teadfastly **T**rusting)

Verse to Remember:
"Our light and momentary troubles are achieving for us an eternal glory that far outweighs them all" (2 Corinthians 4:17, NIV).

Questions of the Day:
• What are some life tests you have experienced?

• What did you gain from those experiences?

• When are you most tempted to sin?

Read Proverbs 16:17 and think about what you should do to avoid unnecessary tests. Write your response below.

- What are the four steps to passing life's tests?

- List the names of all the people who are counting on you to pass your tests, along with the reasons why you won't disappoint them.

DAY 39

D ivine
I nsight
E xposes
T ruth

The good man eats to live, while the evil man lives to eat.

—Proverbs 13:25, TLB

Insight is perception backed by divine intelligence. When you are in tune with God, you know what you know because God tells you. To the receiver, the information is a witness that God speaks to him or her.

Insight is the eye of the H.E.A.R.T. (Higher Empowerment Abides Resourcefully Therein). It gives you the power to see the consequences of an action at the very beginning.

Over the years, my mother has developed keen insight. When I was seventeen years old, my dad bought me my first car, a bright yellow Dodge Colt. One morning my mom told me that she'd had a dream that I was in an accident. She said she saw my car slide into another car, and a third car hit me. She said the accident was pretty bad. She asked me not to drive the car to school for a couple of weeks. I refused. She then asked me to pray for God to protect me. She told me to pray the twenty-third psalm every day for the next couple of weeks and to be extra careful in my driving.

I ignored her warning. A few days later, I left the house and got into my beloved car. I exited our subdivision, turned right, and went a couple of blocks. A dark-blue Fiat Spyder was stopped in front of the entrance of the neighborhood elementary school. The driver was allowing another car to enter the parking lot. When I saw the car, I tapped my brake, but the car would not slow down. I downshifted, but that didn't work either. It had rained the night before and the temperature had dropped, creating a thin, invisible layer of ice on the ground.

I jammed on the brakes, turned the wheel to the left, and slid into the bumper of the Fiat. A big blue Ford station wagon traveling in the opposite direction ran into the front quarter panel of my car on the passenger side. My car spun and was knocked about thirty feet onto the sidewalk. The car was totaled; amazingly, I was not hurt. The accident may have been avoided had I heeded my mom's insight, but I didn't.

Insight exposes truth, and it also exposes lies. Insight is a gift that I believe God has given all those who are seeking the kingdom of God and its righteousness. *Righteousness* means "total dominion of the Spirit within." Jesus is our righteousness. His spirit is within you, if you have accepted him as Lord and submit to him.

"We have the mind of Christ" (1 Corinthians 2:16, NKJV). To the extent that your spiritual diet conforms to the thoughts of Christ, you will realize that you do indeed have the mind of Christ. "Be not conformed to this world, but be ye transformed by the renewing of your mind." Romans 12:2 contrasts two ways of letting our minds become formed.

1. Conformity to the world outside of us.
2. Transformation from within us, which comes about by "casting down imaginations and every high thing that exalteth itself against the knowledge of God, and bringing into captivity every thought to the obedience of Christ" (2 Corinthians 10:5, KJV).

Transformation is a constant diet of renewal. If you were trying to transform an unhealthy body that is suffering from high blood pressure and high cholesterol, you would change your physical diet and you would exercise if you were not already exercising. Instead of eating a hamburger and french fries, you might eat baked chicken, salmon, and vegetables or some other healthy foods low in saturated fat.

If you've ever dieted, you know that such transformation is difficult, especially if you have been eating unhealthily for most of your life. Nevertheless, it is necessary to change your physical diet if you want to avoid the prospect of heart disease or early death. Because you are serious about your health, you train your mind to eat right. You take control and form a habit of eating what is healthy and rejecting foods that are unhealthy.

The same principle applies to your spiritual diet. However, you let Jesus have control of your thoughts. By your spiritual diet, "God is working in you, giving you the desire to obey him and the power to do what pleases him" (Philippians 2:13, NLT). As a result, you experience the abundant life that Jesus said he came to provide for you (John 10:10).

Every thought that comes to mind and that is not in accordance with the Word of God you are to cast down. Many of us find it difficult to cast down ungodly thinking and actions, because we have developed a reverence for things that are not of God. We have made them our F.A.L.S.E. G.O.D.S. (Fear, Anger, Laziness, Sloth, Envy, Greed, Despair, and Stupidity), all of which are forms of fear. They cause us to do the wrong things or to do nothing but wait for the things that we fear to finally happen. As Job said, "What I feared has come upon me" (Job 3:25, NIV).

"God has not given us a spirit of fear, but of power and of love and of sound mind" (2 Timothy 1:7, NKJV). When the devil enters your mind and causes you to imagine the worst, you have the power to cast those negative and limiting imaginings down into hell where they belong.

Love is an action word. And love is the strongest power you have working for you (John 13:35; 1 Peter 4:8). When you love God and align your thoughts with God's Word, God perfects your thoughts. God inspires you to take bold actions. "Perfect love drives out fear" (1 John 4:18, NIV). You will find yourself speaking up, when in the past you would have been afraid to say anything. You will find yourself aggressively pursuing your dreams, when before you were afraid to. A good spiritual diet provides the insight and power to do things that are impossible for mere men and women. It becomes possible for you because you become what you eat. A person who regularly eats high-fat foods becomes fat. A person who gets on God's spiritual diet becomes a spiritual, capable, and maximized being. Such a person can do all things through Christ who strengthens him or her.

As you become more conscious of your spiritual diet, God begins to provide you with a greater depth of perception and insight. God's presence begins to develop in your mind. You will see things that you couldn't see before, and you will know things that you could not have known had God not revealed them to you. Anything negative that you see, you will begin praying so that those things may pass you by if it is the will of God.

Because you are eating the fruit of only the trees from which God wants you to, the devil will no longer be able to cause you to eat the forbidden fruit. God will let you know what the devil wants to do to you before it even happens, just as Jesus did Peter (Luke 22:31). If you are obedient, you will be at least one step ahead of the devil.

A healthy spiritual D.I.E.T. is a must to live a life of G.O.L.D. (God-Ordained Life Development). If you have gotten this far in the book, I trust that you have been spiritually well-fed over the past few weeks. Don't stop. Continue this nourishment as if your life depends on it, because it does. Just as your body is prone to sickness and disease without proper nutrition, so is your soul.

Study your Bible daily. Go to the bookstore and let God lead you to another good book to read. Attend church every Sunday and attend Bible study. Continue to grow, and you will flow in the things of God.

Acronym to Remember: D.I.E.T.
(Divine Insight Exposes Truth)

Verse to Remember:
"The good man eats to live, while the evil man lives to eat" (Proverbs 13:25, TLB).

Questions of the Day:
• What are the two ways that Romans 12:2 contrasts our minds being formed?

- What is transformation to you?

- Through a good spiritual diet, what is God doing through you?

- How conscientious are you about your spiritual diet?

- How conscientious are you about your physical diet and exercise?

DAY 40

T o
H ave
A nd
N ot
K now

Y ields
O ne
U seless

GOD, my God,
I can't thank you enough.

—Psalm 30:12, The Message

Give thanks in all circumstances, for this is God's will for you in Christ Jesus.

—1 Thessalonians 5:18, NIV

One of the best-selling books of all times almost didn't happen. A Methodist pastor wrote a book about positive thinking. He submitted the manuscript to every publisher he could think of. All of them rejected his work. In disgust, he threw the original manuscript away. Without telling him, his wife picked the manuscript out of the trash and submitted it to one more publisher.

That was over fifty years ago. The author was the late Rev. Dr. Norman Vincent Peale. His book, *The Power of Positive Thinking*, is a classic that has been translated into more than fifteen languages and has sold over 7 million copies. It is still in print.

Regardless of how much God pours the divine into one's work, I have found that getting published can be an arduous task. The 140 publishers who all said no to Jack Canfield and Mark Victor Hansen's *Chicken*

Soup for the Soul had no idea their books would generate over a billion dollars in revenue and be in the *Guinness Book of World Records*. Jack and Mark had no idea that God would bless their work so richly either. However, they believed in the power of their "God-idea" and refused to accept rejection. They withdrew the book from their agent, represented themselves, and sold the book to a small publishing house that recognized the value of their "God-idea." When God calls you to do something, "no" is unacceptable. As I mentioned before, "praise" means "to set a price on." Sometimes God will allow you to go through trials to test your faith and to see if you will praise him during challenging times.

As I conclude this book, I recall the day when I felt as if the wind had been kicked out of me. My agent had stirred up some interest with two major publishers in the original book proposal. The acquisitions editors at both publishing houses believed they had a winner. However, the publishing boards at those companies did not agree. I felt down, and I needed comforting.

Jesus said, "The Counselor, the Holy Spirit, whom the Father will send in my name, will teach you all things and remind you of everything I have said to you" (John 14:26, NIV). After I sulked for a day, I thanked God for using me to get God's message out. I thanked God for blessing me with one of the best literary agents in the business, Dave Robie at BigScore Productions.

"Thank you" is one of the highest forms of praise. In your darkest hour you can see your L.I.G.H.T. (Life Is in God's Hand's Totally). The outcome is not up to you or anyone else. God has the final word. After thanking God, I asked, "Lord, what should we do now?"

The planned title was *101 Acronyms to Heal the Soul*. We changed the name of the book to *40 Days to a Life of G.O.L.D.* and changed the entire format. God also reminded me of a dream I'd had while writing the book. In the dream I was flying a plane and I landed prematurely and found myself in a foreign territory. After the dream, God spoke to me in a meditation and said, "Don't land." When we are doing something that we know God has ordained for us to do, it is important that we continue to move forward, using our past for instruction and our future for construction. What appears to be F.A.I.L.U.R.E. is simply Forward Actions

In Life Unfolding Rewarding Experiences. God is setting you up for a blessing that you will know came from heaven.

If you become discouraged and give up, you abort the mission. Norman Vincent Peale was much closer than he realized to getting a publisher for *The Power of Positive Thinking* when he gave up. He was fortunate that God had given him a wife who believed in him and in what God was doing through him. She picked the work up when he dropped it in the trash and sent it out again. The rest is history.

I was reminded that part of my divine assignment is this book. God manifests glory in your life when you trust in the Lord and move forward with your divine assignment in spite of obstacles.

People who cannot see the blessings of God in their life are ungrateful. Because they lack gratitude, the concept of G.O.L.D. escapes them. Too often we feel that others need to validate us or that what we have is of no value.

This is what the LORD says:
"Cursed is the one who trusts in man,
    who depends on flesh for his strength
    and whose heart turns away from the Lord.
He will be like a bush in wastelands;
    he will not see prosperity when it comes."

—Jeremiah 17:5, NIV

As discussed earlier, the widow in 2 Kings 4 had abundant wealth and didn't know it: "One day the wife of a man from the guild of prophets called out to Elisha, 'Your servant my husband is dead. You well know what a good man he was, devoted to GOD. And now the man to whom he was in debt is on his way to collect by taking my two children as slaves'" (2 Kings 4:1, The Message).

No one can give you anything that God has not already given you. Elisha asked a question because he wanted the woman to look within her house (her mind) and recall what God had already blessed her with. "Elisha said, 'I wonder how can I be of help. Tell me, what do you have in your house?'" (2 Kings 4:2, The Message).

"'Your servant has nothing there at all,' she said, 'except a little oil'" (2 Kings 4:2, NIV). The oil represents divine ideas. The woman had a

"God-anointed idea" in her mind that she didn't believe in. God used Elisha as a counselor. He used an inside-out approach and guided her into turning her idea into monetary substance. She had to first look inside to see the "God-idea" she had sitting in the cupboard of her mind.

He then directed her to look outside and around her for resources. "He said, 'Go, borrow vessels at large for yourself from all your neighbors, even empty vessels; do not get a few. And you shall go in and shut the door behind you and your sons, and pour out into all these vessels, and you shall set aside what is full'" (2 Kings 4:3-4, NASB).

If your idea is to write a book, a publisher is just a resource. If your God-idea is to record music, a recording company is just a resource. If your divine idea is to own your own business, banks and investors are just resources. You should not approach just a few of them and then give up after experiencing rejection. You are to approach many until you find the right one. You believe that God gave you this assignment. Your carrying out the work will provide your sustenance. As Jesus said, "My meat is to do the will of him that sent me, and to finish his work" (John 4:34, KJV).

Returning to the story of Elisha and the widow, we discover that "she did what he said. She locked the door behind her and her sons; as they brought the containers to her, she filled them" (2 Kings 4:5, The Message). In other words, she and her sons closed the door on the crisis they were in and focused on the work that was at hand.

When all the jugs and bowls were full, she said to one of her sons, "Another jug, please."

He said, "That's it. There are no more jugs."

—2 Kings 4:5-6, The Message

The flow stopped.

The word *affluence*, in its Latin root *affleur*, means "to flow." The flow of divine ideas stops the moment we give in to fear. The woman panicked. There were no more resources to contact on her list.

"She went and told the story to the man of God. He said, 'Go sell the oil and make good on your debts. Live, both you and your sons, on what is left'" (2 Kings 4:7, The Message).

An attitude of gratitude causes you to focus on God and God's goodness. It causes you to say, "Thank you, Jesus." You appreciate it when God shows you favor with those whose resources you are seeking. You also appreciate it when it appears that those entities don't show favor to you.

With over 90 million books sold, I can assure you that Jack Canfield and Mark Victor Hansen are thanking God all the way to the bank that their work was rejected by the 140 publishers who did not see the value of acquiring their work and promoting them. And I am sure the publishing boards of those companies regret that they let such an opportunity get away from them. Persistence pays off.

God's remnant are those individuals set aside for God's purpose. The majority of people are not remnant people. If you are a remnant person and God is doing a remnant work through you, do not expect everyone to see the value of your divine ideas. Not everyone has prophetic insight. I believe my agent and the acquisitions editors at the publishing houses who saw the value of this book had prophetic insight when they read it.

In spite of all rejection and disappointment, press on and pray to God daily. Rejection is just a testing of your faith. "My brethren, count it all joy when you fall into various trials, knowing that the testing of your faith produces patience. But let patience have its perfect work, that you may be perfect and complete, lacking nothing" (James 1:2-4, NKJV). Don't give up when you experience rejection. Pause and ask God what your next step should be. Don't move without God, and always say, T.H.A.N.K. Y.O.U. (To Have And Not Know Yields One Useless). God is your provider!

Acronym to Remember: **T.H.A.N.K. Y.O.U.**
(**To Have And Not Know Yields One Useless**)

Verse to Remember:
"Enter with the password: Thank you!" (Psalm 100:4, The Message).

Questions of the Day:
• In addition to the name Jesus, what is the password to the glory of God?

- According to Jeremiah 17:5, what is the person who puts his trust in humankind?

- From whom should you seek validation?

- What are some ideas that God has placed inside you?

- What are you going to do with them?

- Sometimes rejection is just a testing of your faith. What are you going to do if the ideas that God has given to you are rejected, and why?

- Think of a time in your life when you felt like giving up but didn't. What was the outcome of your perseverance?

- Reflect on Romans 8:28: "And we who know that in all things God works for the good of those who love him, who have been called according to his purpose" (NIV). Reflecting on your past successes and seeming failures, how does this Scripture apply to your life?

- List some things for which you are thankful. Have you said "Thank you!" to God today?

CONTINUING FORWARD

The number 40 is the biblical number of probation. It is a period of trial and testing. Just before Jesus went on to fulfill his purpose for being on this earth, he was led by the Spirit into the wilderness for 40 days to be tested. Jesus had the fortitude to weather his probationary period without allowing the devil to cause him to err.

Jesus passed his test by submitting himself to God. Because he submitted, it was easy for the Holy Spirit to lead him. Had he not submitted, the Holy Spirit could not have prepared him to overcome the challenges that lay ahead of him.

As you prepare yourself, you will discover that through Christ Jesus you have the T.A.L.E.N.T.S. (Tools, Ability/Anointing, Love; Everything Needed To Succeed) to overcome the challenges that are before you, including those in your daily life. Your acts of preparation will prompt the progression of God's blessings in your life and in the lives of those for whom you are responsible, such as your spouse, children, and subordinates at work. Those to whom you are responsible, such as your employer and even your customers, will also benefit.

How do you prepare yourself? You prepare yourself through the reading of God's Word. To meet the challenges in the wilderness, Jesus quoted the Word of God to the devil, as well as to himself, and demonstrated his submission to God by acting upon those words. To meet *your* challenges you will need to follow Jesus' example. This requires that you gain a working knowledge of God's Word.

As suggested on Day 35, read at least three chapters of your Bible each day. Studying God's Word is a prerequisite of preparation. The process of becoming fully prepared is a matter of doing God's will and acting upon God's Word. This will demonstrate to God, you, the devil, and others that you are indeed submitted to God. Your acts of preparation will prompt the progression of God's blessings in your life.

I also suggest that you seek wisdom and understanding. Wisdom comes from sincere honor of God and God's Word. Understanding is the result of keeping away from morally corrupt ways and lifestyles. "And [God] said to humankind, 'Truly, the fear of the Lord, that is wisdom; and to depart from evil is understanding'" (Job 28:28, NRSV). "For although they knew God, they neither glorified him as God nor gave thanks to him, but their thinking became futile and their foolish hearts were darkened. Although they claimed to be wise, they became fools" (Romans 1:21-22, NIV). Turning from God results in God's judgment and wrath. Submission to God, however, is a choice that leads to all success and happiness.

Submission also requires that you serve others as if you are serving God. God blessed Solomon with wisdom because Solomon realized he needed wisdom to best serve God's children as king. In whatever it is that God has ordained you to do, you will need wisdom to realize your full potential. Because wisdom is lacking in our lives, many of us miss our destinies. We take foolish courses of action and end up some place other than where God intended for us to be.

My son, do not forget my teaching,
   but keep my commands in your heart,
for they will prolong your life many years
   and bring you prosperity.
Let love and faithfulness never leave you;
   bind them around your neck,
   write them on the tablet of your heart.
Then you will win favor and a good name
   in the sight of God and man.
Trust in the LORD with all your heart
   and lean not on your own understanding;
in all your ways acknowledge him,
   and he will make your paths straight.
Do not be wise in your own eyes;
   fear the LORD and shun evil.
This will bring health to your body
   and nourishment to your bones.

   —Proverbs 3:1-8, NIV

If you feel you lack wisdom, I encourage you to ask God for it, and he will give it to you generously if you have a sincere reverence for him, believe in him, and follow his Word. "If any of you is lacking in wisdom, ask God, who gives to all generously and ungrudgingly, and it will be given you" (James 1:5, NRSV). Jesus directs us, "Ask, and it will be given you; search, and you will find; knock, and the door will be opened for you. For everyone who searches finds, and for everyone who knocks, the door will be opened" (Matthew 7:7-8, NRSV).

In addition to your scheduled Bible reading, I encourage you to read a chapter in the morning of Proverbs and a chapter in the evening from Psalms. I believe Solomon was the wealthiest man in the world because he was the wisest man in the world. Godly wisdom is a blessing of the Lord that brings forth wealth. "The blessing of the LORD brings wealth, and he adds no trouble to it" (Proverbs 10:22, NIV). Wealth is not just money. When you flow in the things of God, you will find that God provides for all of your needs. "And my God will meet all your needs according to his glorious riches in Christ Jesus" (Philippians 4:19, NIV).

I have enjoyed sharing time with you over these past forty days, and I hope that our relationship will continue. I invite you to keep in touch. E-mail me at ed@edgrayspeaks.com.

Together, we prepare ourselves and continue forward.

Enthusiastically,
Ed Gray